SPECTRUM®

Reading

Grade 4

Published by Spectrum®
an imprint of Carson-Dellosa Publishing LLC
Greensboro, NC 27425 USA

Spectrum®
An imprint of Carson-Dellosa Publishing LLC
P.O. Box 35665
Greensboro, NC 27425 USA

ISBN 978-1-4838-1217-5

11-189197811

Table of Contents

A Morning in Maine

What would you like to see if you traveled to Maine?

1   "Cameron!" called Grandpa. "Are you awake yet? It's almost eight o'clock. We're wasting the day!" Grandpa stood in the doorway. He wore faded blue jeans, a checkered shirt, and a big grin.

2   "Grandpa," groaned Cameron, "it's the first day of my vacation. I never get up this early when I'm on vacation."

3   "That's because you don't live in Maine," replied Grandpa, opening the shutters and letting the sun spill across the bed. "There is so much to do here that you won't want to miss a thing. Besides, I'm making blueberry pancakes. If you don't get up soon, they may not last."

4   "Okay. The pancakes convinced me, Grandpa," said Cameron, swinging his legs out of bed.

5   "I had a feeling they might," Grandpa chuckled.

6   Over blueberry pancakes with warm maple syrup, Cameron and Grandpa discussed their plans for the day. "I'd like to do some exploring this morning," said Cameron, taking a gulp of milk. "Does that path next to the cabin go straight down to the beach? And how do you get to that little island with the pine trees? Do you think we could catch some fish for dinner?"

7   Grandpa laughed. "I thought there were a few things you might want to do today instead of sleep. Why don't we go for a walk on the beach after breakfast? Later, we can go fishing on the island."

8   "Sounds good to me," said Cameron excitedly.

9   Cameron and Grandpa did the dishes. Then, they put on some old sneakers and followed the sandy path to the beach. The air felt crisp and warm. There was not a cloud in the sky.

10   Cameron was a few steps ahead of his grandfather. He stopped to look at a pool of water that had formed between some rocks. "Look at this, Grandpa!" shouted Cameron. "It's like a miniature ocean."

11   Cameron crouched down to get a better look. Grandpa peered over his shoulder. "There are so many little creatures in there," Cameron said. "How did they get there?"

12   "It's a tide pool, Cameron," said Grandpa. "You'll see them all along this beach. They are my favorite thing to look for on my morning walks. You see, when the tide goes out, water gets caught in shallow pools. It's a pretty neat way to see a little slice of ocean life."

13   Cameron nodded. "This is very cool," he said. "If we had stuff like this at home, I might actually want to get up early. I have a feeling this is going to be a great vacation!"

Write **T** before the sentences that are true. Write **F** before the sentences that are false.

1. _F_ Cameron is visiting his grandpa in Massachusetts.

2. _F_ Cameron wakes up before Grandpa does.

3. _T_ Grandpa makes blueberry pancakes for breakfast.

4. _T_ Cameron and Grandpa plan to go fishing in the afternoon.

5. _F_ Cameron and Grandpa have to drive to get to the beach.

6. _F_ Grandpa finds the tide pool before Cameron does.

7. Name one thing Cameron wants to do when he goes exploring.

   Cameron wants to go fishing

Write the words from the story that have the meanings below.

8. changed someone's mind

   Convinced me to get out of bed.
   Par. 4

9. talked about

   Disscused plans for the day
   Par. 6

10. very small

    A pool of water w/ creatures
    Par. 10

11. ocean water that moves in and out several times a day

    Tide
    Par. 12

12. not deep

    Tide pool
    Par. 12

13. This story is told in the (first-person, third-person) point of view.

14. Do you think Cameron lives near a beach? Why or why not?

    I think he lives near a beach because
    he visited the Beach and Maine is
    surounded by the Atlantic Ocean.

A Slice of Ocean Life

What do you think you might see in a tide pool?

1   You might think that the ocean is the only place in nature to find sea creatures. But if you visit the beaches of the northeast United States, you might get to see all kinds of ocean life in the miniature worlds of tide pools.

2   Tide pools form when the tide goes out and ocean water is trapped in rocky hollows near the shore. Many different types of plants and animals live in these pools. The one thing they have in common is that they must be strong. It is not easy to survive in an environment that changes often.

3   High-level pools are shallow. They are the most difficult types of pools for animals to live in. The sun causes some of the water in these shallow pools to evaporate, or dry up. That makes the water even saltier than the ocean. On the other hand, when there is a lot of rain, high-level pools lose much of their saltiness. This can also be hard for sea creatures to survive.

4   Some animals have shells that keep them from drying out in the sun. A barnacle has a soft, slippery body that is covered with a hard shell made of tiny plates. Barnacles attach themselves to rocks. When sea water washes over them, barnacles open up their plates. They use their legs to trap small bits of food from the water.

5   It is a bit easier for sea creatures to live in mid-level tide pools. The water is deeper there. The tide washes over them several times a day, so they do not become too dry. Creatures like the starfish and the sea urchin live in mid-level pools. Their sticky tube feet help them cling to rocks. This keeps them from being pulled out to sea by big waves.

6   Sea anemones, which look like seaweed, also live in mid-level tide pools. An animal that gets stung by the tentacles of a sea anemone finds out very quickly that it is not a plant.

7   Low-level tide pools often contain forests of kelp, a type of brown seaweed. The kelp provides a home or serves as food for many types of sea animals, such as small fish, worms, crabs, sponges, and sea urchins. Ocean animals are not the only ones who find a good use for kelp. People use it as an ingredient in ice cream.

8   The next time you have a chance to stroll along the ocean shore, be sure to keep your eyes open. You just might get to peek through a window into the world of underwater animals.

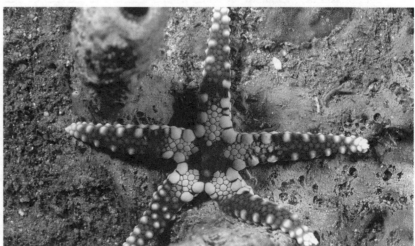

Circle the word that best completes each sentence and write it on the line.

1. Plants and animals must be _____ to survive in a tide pool.

   weak   large   (strong)

2. When water dries up, it _____.

   (evaporates)   dies   melts

3. Starfish and sea urchins have sticky _____.

   backs   eyes   (feet)

4. Which type of tide pool is most difficult for animals to live in?

   High level tide pools because the Sun ||
   causes water to dry up.
5. What is one way humans use kelp? _And saltiness_

   Food for Ocean Animals and ingrediant for
   Ice cream.
6. Check the reason the author probably wrote this story.

   _____ to entertain the reader

   _✓_ to give some facts about tide pools

   _____ to teach people about ocean tides

7. What is the main idea of paragraph 3?

   To tell you about High level pools

8. A barnacle is a _Animals that go in high level pools_.

9. Why are mid-level tide pools easier for animals to live in?

   because there's more water which
   means more space

10. Have you ever seen a tide pool? If so, describe it. If not, tell what you would hope
    to find in it.

    I've never seen a tide pool in
    life but I would like to see a Star Fish

Grandpa's Light Show

What would you think if you saw colored lights moving across the night sky?

1   Cameron and Grandpa were preparing for Cameron's parents to arrive for the weekend. First, they opened all the windows so the cabin would smell like the fresh ocean air. Grandpa did three loads of laundry, and Cameron helped him hang the sheets to dry on the clothesline. Then, they picked two buckets of blueberries. "Enough to turn our fingers and our tongues blue!" said Grandpa.

2   It was just before dinnertime when Cameron's parents arrived. They were exhausted from their long drive and ready to relax.

3   "Wait until you see what we have planned for dinner," said Cameron, hugging his parents. He gave them only a few minutes to change their clothes and unpack before he led them down the path to the beach. Grandpa had already started a small fire in the fire pit.

4   "I had no idea you two were such good fishermen and cooks!" said Mom when she sampled the fish and the roasted corn. "This tastes wonderful! It reminds me of summers in Maine when I was a girl," she said, smiling and patting Grandpa on the knee.

5   "It gets even better, I hear," said Dad. "When's dessert?"

6   Mom, Dad, Grandpa, and Cameron were eating their blueberry sundaes on the porch when streaks of green, yellow, and purple shot across the sky.

7   "Did you see that?" shouted Cameron, jumping out of his chair. "What do you think that was? It looked like it could have been a spaceship or something!"

8   Mom began to laugh. "That," she said, "was the perfect ending to a perfect day."

9   "Those are the northern lights, Cameron," said Grandpa. "I'm so glad you got a chance to see them. Spring and fall are usually a much better time than summer to see them in Maine."

10   "Look, there they go again," said Dad, pointing to a flickering of pink and pale green light over the water.

11   "But what are they?" asked Cameron.

12   "I guess you could call them a colored light show in the night sky," said Grandpa. "You can only see them in the parts of the world that have high latitudes, which means the areas are closer to the poles. Tonight is a perfect night to see the northern lights because it is clear and moonless."

13   Cameron sat back down in his chair and picked up his bowl of ice cream. "Grandpa, I think I just might have to move to Maine. There is definitely too much to see here on just one vacation!"

Write **C** before the groups of words that describe Cameron and **G** before the groups of words that describe Grandpa.

1. _____ said that spring and fall are better times for seeing the northern lights

2. _____ thought the northern lights were a spaceship

3. _____ started a fire in the fire pit on the beach

4. _____ wants to move to Maine

5. _____ said blueberries would turn their fingers blue

Write **T** before the sentences that are true. Write **F** before the sentences that are false.

6. _____ Cameron and Grandpa bought some blueberries at the store.

7. _____ Grandpa picked up Cameron's parents at the airport.

8. _____ Dinner reminds Mom of summers in Maine when she was little.

9. _____ Grandpa has never seen the northern lights before.

10. _____ The northern lights are usually seen only in places with high latitudes.

11. Name one thing Cameron and Grandpa do to prepare for Cameron's parents.

_____

_____

Check the meaning of the underlined word in each sentence.

12. Cameron and Grandpa <u>picked</u> two buckets of blueberries.

_____ chose

_____ gathered

13. Cameron thought the northern lights <u>looked</u> like a spaceship in the sky.

_____ appeared

_____ stared

14. You can see the northern lights in parts of the world that are closer to the <u>poles</u>.

_____ long, thin sticks

_____ the most northern and southern ends of Earth

Mysterious Lights

What do you think causes the northern lights?

1   Many years ago, people who saw waves of color dance across the sky at night were frightened. Some groups of people made up legends to explain what today is known as the northern lights, or *aurora borealis* (uh-ROAR-uh bore-ee-A-LUSS). Aurora was the Roman goddess of dawn, or early morning. The word *boreal* means *north* in Latin, so *aurora borealis* means *northern lights*.

2   The sun gives off particles that are filled with energy. Large groups of these particles travel together. They are called *solar wind*. The particles travel through space at hundreds of miles per second. Even traveling that fast, it still takes several days for the particles to reach Earth. When the solar wind gets close to Earth, it moves toward the two magnetic poles, the North Pole and the South Pole.

3   When the solar particles get close to Earth, they become trapped in Earth's atmosphere. They collide, or run into, gases in the atmosphere. The energy that is made in that collision creates light.

When lots of these collisions happen at the same time, northern lights can be seen from Earth. The northern lights are harmless, but it can be frightening to see the sky fill with flashing colored lights if you do not know what they are.

4   As far as scientists can tell, the northern lights do not make any sounds that people on Earth can hear. Even so, if you live in a place where the northern lights can be seen, you might notice problems with your television, radio, or cell phone every once in a while. The energy created by solar wind in the Earth's atmosphere can get in the way of sound waves and pictures that travel through the air to your TV or radio.

5   The northern lights are truly amazing, especially the first time you see them. Even in the highest latitudes, the lowest section of the lights are still 40 miles above Earth. The northern lights stretch up about six hundred miles into the atmosphere. Imagine what a light show you would see if you were an astronaut looking down on the northern lights from space.

Circle the word that best completes each sentence and write it on the line.

1. Some people made up _____ to explain the lights they saw in the sky.

   paintings   legends   experiments

2. Solar particles and _____ collide in Earth's atmosphere to create the northern lights.

   gases   light   ice

3. Scientists do not think the northern lights make any _____.

   explosions   steam   sounds

4. In Roman myths, who was Aurora?

   _____

5. Toward which two areas of Earth does solar wind move?

   _____

6. About how far away from Earth is the lowest section of the northern lights?

   _____

7. Check the sentence that best states the main idea of the selection.

   _____ The northern lights are amazing the first time you see them.

   _____ Collisions of solar particles create lights in the night sky.

   _____ The northern lights are also called *aurora borealis*.

8. Why do you think the northern lights can be frightening?

   _____

   _____

9. Why do the northern lights sometimes interfere with TV or cell phone reception?

   _____

   _____

The Land of the Northern Lights

What legends have you heard that explain something in nature?

1 Many years ago, there lived a Wabanaki chief. He had only one child, a son. The chief often worried about his son. He did not see the boy run and play with other children in the village. Still, the boy would disappear for hours at a time. His parents were never quite sure where he would go.

2 One day, the chief saw his son follow a milky white path up into the sky. The chief followed his son on the path but lost sight of him when he arrived in a strange and unfamiliar country.

3 "Where am I?" the chief wondered aloud, as he stood looking around the strange land where everything was lit by a dim white light.

4 An old man with wrinkled skin and kind eyes heard the chief. "You are in the Land of the Northern Lights," replied the old man.

5 "But how did I get here?" asked the chief. "Where has my son gone?"

6 The old man placed his hand on the chief's shoulder. "You came here the same way I did," he said. "You followed the trail of the Milky Way. Your son comes often to play with our children."

7 "Please take me to him," said the chief.

8 The two men walked along until they came to a group of braves playing ball. The chief had never seen children playing ball before. He watched excitedly as they ran and laughed and tossed the ball through the air. Each brave wore a belt made of a rainbow. As they leaped and ran after the ball, lights in the colors of the rainbow swirled around them.

9 For a few moments, the chief could only watch as the children chased the ball and threw it in the air. Shimmering lights in blue, green, red, gold, and purple danced across the milky white sky. The brightest lights came from the chief's son, who moved quickly and easily among the other braves.

10 When the game had ended, the boy noticed his father watching him. "You are not angry with me, are you?" he asked the chief.

11 "No, I am not angry," answered the chief, putting one arm around the boy's shoulder. "But it is time to go back to our village now. Perhaps you can teach the children to play the games you have played here."

12 The old man sent two large birds to carry the chief and his son along the path of the Milky Way to their village. From that day on, whenever the chief and his son saw the northern lights, they thought of the children laughing and playing ball in the sky, the colors from their rainbow belts swirling around them.

1. Number the events below from **1** to **5** to show the order in which they happened in the story.

   2 Whenever the chief and his son saw the northern lights, they thought of the children playing ball.

   3 The chief and the old man watched the braves play ball.

   1 The boy's parents were worried about him.

   4 The boy asked the chief if he was angry.

   5 The boy followed the trail of the Milky Way.

2. The boy's parents were worried about him because _they never saw him play._

3. How did the boy and the chief get to the Land of the Northern Lights?

   By following the Milky Way path.

4. What were the belts the braves wore made of?

   Rainbow

5. What do you think the boy taught the children in the Wabanaki village when he got home?

   the game they were playing with the Braves

6. This story is a legend. What elements make a legend different from a regular story?

   That Legends are something someone believes in

7. What natural event does this legend explain?

   Rainbows, and Nordern Lights

8. What does the word *brave* mean in paragraph 8? Use the context of the story to help you answer.

   Each young child of the old man

A Mancala Morning

Have you ever played a game from another country?

1   On Saturday morning, Madison and her friends Drew and Kiona were planning to go for a bike ride. They were waiting for Malaika, the high school exchange student from Africa who was staying with Madison's family.

2   Madison, Drew, and Kiona had a snack while they waited for Malaika to come home from the library. Madison was just pouring some popcorn into a big bowl when she heard a rumble of thunder.

3   "Uh-oh," said Drew, looking out the kitchen window. The sky was turning darker, and the wind blew dry leaves across the backyard. "It looks like today might not be the best day for a bike ride."

4   Suddenly, the front door slammed. Malaika came inside and put down her backpack. Her hair was ruffled from the wind. Tiny drops of rain dotted her glasses.

5   "Hi, Malaika!" called Madison. "What's it like outside?"

6   "It looks like a big storm is rolling in," said Malaika, wiping her glasses on the corner of her shirt.

7   Madison sighed. "Now we have nothing to do this afternoon," she said. "I really wanted to go for a bike ride. It's going to start getting cold out soon. This might have been the last weekend to ride until spring!"

8   Malaika laughed. "My brothers, sisters, and I never had bikes," she said, "but we still had plenty of things to keep us occupied on rainy days. Have you ever played the African game called *Mancala*?"

9   "I've never heard of it," said Madison, shaking her head.

10   "I haven't either," added Kiona.

11   "I played that at camp last year," said Drew. "It was one of the games in our game room. But how can we play without a board?"

12   "I know just the thing," said Malaika. "All we need is an egg carton, some dried beans, and some markers."

13   Madison and Drew gathered the materials. Then, Malaika and Kiona put red dots on 24 beans and green dots on the other 24 beans.

14   "Now what?" asked Kiona.

15   "Well, we need to have two teams. Since Drew and I have both played before, we'll be on different teams. What should we name the teams?"

16   "Let's see," said Kiona. "Drew and I will be the Mancala All-Stars." She grinned. "As long as you can be all-stars without having won anything yet."

17   "Malaika and I will be the 5Ms," said Madison. "That stands for Madison and Malaika the Marvelous Mancala Masters!"

18   "Are you ready to learn the rules and play the first game?" asked Malaika.

19   "Sure," said Kiona. "I can't wait to earn our name."

20   "Not if we can help it!" shouted Madison and Malaika together.

A **fact** is something that can be proven to be true. An **opinion** is what a person believes. It may or may not be true. Write **F** before the sentences that are facts. Write **O** before the sentences that are opinions.

1. _F_ Madison's friends are named Drew and Kiona.

2. _O_ Thunderstorms are exciting.

3. _F_ Madison put some popcorn in a bowl.

4. _F_ Drew doesn't know how they will play Mancala without a board.

5. _O_ Drew and Kiona will win the game.

6. _O_ Mancala All-Stars is a great name for the winning team.

7. Check the sentence that best states the main idea of the story.

_____ Madison gets bored when it rains.

_✓_ On a rainy afternoon, Malaika teaches some friends how to play an African game.

_____ Malaika tells her friends about her life in Africa.

8. Where did Drew learn how to play Mancala?

At a camp

9. What does the team name the *5Ms* stand for?

Madison and Malaika the Marvelous Mancala Masters

10. What materials will the girls need to play Mancala?

Egg carton, dry beans and 2 markers

11. A **cause** makes something happen. An **effect** is what happens as a result. Write one cause and one effect from the story.

Cause: _It started raining so they couldn't bike thing_

Effect: _They had to play a game_

12. Describe a game you like to play on rainy afternoons.

Bellz

_____

It's All a Game

What are some of your favorite games to play?

1 Games from all around the world can be fun and simple to play. Some of the games might be similar to ones you have played many times before. Others may be new to you. The one thing you can be sure of is that you will enjoy getting a glimpse of how children in countries around the world like to play.

2 Many countries have a version of the game of jacks. In the United States, it is played with a small rubber ball and 15 star-shaped metal pieces. The object of the game is to pick up a certain number of jacks in one hand on the first bounce of the ball. There are many variations of this game. In Brazil, it is called *Cinco Marias,* or Five Marias, and it is played with pebbles instead of jacks. Smooth, flat stones and two to four players are all you need to play.

3 Another interesting game is the Chinese tangram. It is a puzzle that has been enjoyed in China for more than two hundred years. It might appear to be a simple game, but it is more complex than it seems. You begin with a square of paper that has been divided into seven pieces: five triangles, a square, and a rhombus. The goal is to make as many pictures as possible using the pieces. You can make pictures of animals, people, objects, or things in nature. It is possible to make more than 1,500 images with the seven pieces in a tangram!

Square cut into the seven shapes needed for Chinese tangrams

4 Have you ever seen a group of people kicking around a small, colorful footbag? *Takraw* is a popular game in Thailand. Traditionally, the ball was made of rattan, or a hard, basketlike material. Today, the ball is usually made of hard plastic. The players stand in a group and try to pass the ball back and forth to one another without allowing it to touch the ground. Does this sound too simple? The trick to the game is that you can use only your head, shoulders, feet, and legs, not your arms or hands.

5 The next time you get together with your friends to play a game, think about trying a game from another country. You might find something familiar, or you might find a brand-new pastime.

bird flying

sailboat

Circle the word that best completes each sentence and write it on the line.

1. The Chinese tangram is ___harder___ than it seems.

   easier   older   (harder)

2. In the past, the takraw ball was usually made of ___rattan___.

   plastic   rubber   (rattan)

3. You cannot use your ___hands___ to hit the ball in takraw.

   feet   shoulders   (hands)

4. Check the sentence that best states the main idea of the story.

   _____ *Takraw* is a popular game in Thailand.

   _____ The Chinese tangram puzzle is not as easy as it may seem.

   __✓__ It can be fun and interesting to play games from all around the world.

5. How many shapes is the paper divided into in a tangram?

   ___7___

6. What rule of the game makes takraw difficult to play?

   You can only use your Head, shoulders, feet, and Legs. Although you can't let it touch the ground

Write **J** before the words that describe the United States' version of the game of jacks.
Write **T** before the words that describe Chinese tangram.

7. __J__ played with metal pieces

8. __T__ possible to make more than 1,500 images

9. __T__ begins with a square divided into seven shapes

10. __J__ exists in many variations

11. What is the main idea of paragraph 3?

    To introduce you to a chinese tangram. How to Play, What it is.

12. What is one thing that all the games mentioned in the story have in common?

    _____

    _____

Birthday Breakfast

Have you ever made a surprise meal for someone?

1   "Malaika!" whispered Madison into the early morning darkness. Malaika rolled over in her bed, but she didn't wake up. "Malaika!" whispered Madison again, this time gently shaking the girl's shoulder. "Are you awake?"

2   "What's wrong, Madison?" asked Malaika, sitting straight up in bed.

3   "Nothing. Today is Mom's birthday. Dad and I are going to make her a surprise breakfast of pancakes and eggs. Do you want to help?"

4   Malaika stretched and grinned. "I would love to help, Madison. I've never made pancakes before, and I don't think I've ever eaten American-style eggs. Besides, your mom definitely deserves a birthday surprise!"

5   "Great!" said Madison. "We'll meet you downstairs in about 15 minutes."

6   When Malaika joined Madison in the kitchen, she was assembling the breakfast ingredients. Madison was still wearing her favorite pink pajamas. Her fuzzy white slippers peeked out below her pajama pants like two small rabbits. Dad was dressed for the day, but he didn't look quite awake yet. He sat at the kitchen table sipping coffee from a large mug.

7   "Malaika, I need your help. Dad and I are both terrible at cracking eggs without getting the shells in the batter. Can you break the eggs?"

8   "Sure, Madison. I can even show you how I do it. You just have to give the egg a good crack on the side of the bowl. If you do it too lightly, you have to tap the egg several times. Then, the shell cracks into small pieces," said Malaika.

9   Dad nodded. "That's what Madison's mom always tells us, but we just don't seem to have the touch."

10   "I'm going to try it this time, Dad," said Madison.

11   Madison successfully cracked the eggs into the pan. "I did it!" she cheered.

12   "Shhhh!" said Dad and Malaika.

13   "Oops," said Madison. "I forgot Mom was still sleeping."

14   The rest of the preparation went smoothly. Malaika flipped pancakes while Dad squeezed fresh orange juice and Madison scrambled the eggs. At the last minute, Madison grabbed a fake flower from an arrangement in the living room. She added it to Mom's breakfast tray.

15   "That's what I call a team effort," said Dad. Madison and Malaika agreed.

16   "This will be the best eggshell-free birthday breakfast Mom ever had!" said Madison.

Write **T** before the sentences that are true. Write **F** before the sentences that are false.

1. _____ Madison wakes up Malaika because she is hungry.

2. _____ Madison's favorite pajamas are pink.

3. _____ Malaika has not made pancakes before.

4. _____ Mom helps everyone make pancakes and eggs for breakfast.

5. Do you think Madison will ask Dad and Malaika to help her the next time she wants to plan a surprise? Why or why not?

_____

_____

6. Madison and her dad don't like cracking eggs because _____

_____.

Circle the word that best completes each sentence and write it on the line.

7. Madison's idea for making a surprise breakfast was a _____.

   mistake   success   failure

8. Dad thinks that he, Madison, and Malaika work well as a _____.

   team   business   surprise

9. Paragraph 6 contains a simile, a comparison that uses *like* or *as*. Write the simile on the line, and then tell what two things are being compared.

_____

_____

10. What is Malaika's advice for cracking an egg?

_____

11. Which adjective best describes Malaika?

_____ irritable   _____ helpful   _____ nervous

12. Have you ever surprised someone with a meal you made? If so, tell about it. If not, tell what you would make.

_____

_____

Plenty of Pancakes

Have you ever followed a recipe before?

Before you begin:

- Never use the stove without an adult's supervision.

- Always remember to keep the handle of the skillet turned in so you cannot accidentally bump into it.

- Be sure to wash your hands with soap and hot water after you touch the raw eggs.

Perfect Pancakes

1 cup flour
1 tablespoon sugar
2 teaspoons baking soda
$\frac{1}{4}$ teaspoon salt

1 egg
1 cup milk
2 tablespoons oil

1   Here are some other things you will need: a measuring cup, a teaspoon, a tablespoon, a small bowl, a medium-sized bowl, a wooden spoon, cooking spray, a skillet, a spatula, AND a big appetite.

2   First, mix together the dry ingredients in a medium-sized bowl. Then, mix the milk, egg, and oil together in a small bowl. Make a well, or hole, in the middle of the dry ingredients. Pour the egg mixture into the well. Stir the batter only until it is moist. It should still look lumpy. (If you stir it too long, the pancakes will be tough instead of fluffy.)

3   Coat a skillet with cooking spray and heat it over medium heat. When the skillet is hot, pour in enough batter to make a circle about the size of your fist. Then, tilt the skillet slightly to let the batter spread out and form a bigger circle.

4   When the edges turn light brown and start to bubble, use a spatula to flip the pancake.

5   Serve the pancakes with butter and warm maple syrup. This recipe makes about 8–10 pancakes.

Banana Akara
(African Banana Fritters)

6 very ripe bananas
1 cup flour
$\frac{1}{4}$ cup granulated sugar

$\frac{1}{4}$ cup water
1 teaspoon nutmeg

6   Here are some other things you will need: a measuring cup, a teaspoon, a fork, a small bowl, a large bowl, cooking spray, a skillet, and a spatula.

7   Peel the bananas, and place them in the large bowl. Mash the bananas with a fork. Then, add the flour and stir until blended.

8   Mix together the water and sugar in a small bowl to make a syrup. Then, add the nutmeg to the syrup. Add the syrup to the banana mixture, and mix well. If it is thicker than pancake batter, add a bit more water.

9   Coat a skillet with cooking spray and heat it over medium heat. When the skillet is hot, pour in a small amount of the mixture.

10   Use a spatula to turn the fritter when the edges begin to turn golden brown. This recipe makes about 24 small banana fritters.

1. Check the reason the author probably wrote this story.

    _____ to show you how to become a chef

    _____ to tell about how to make different types of pancakes

    _____ to explain some important rules to remember when you are cooking

2. Number the sentences below to show the order in which you should do each step when you make banana akara.

    _____ Mash the bananas with a fork.

    _____ Flip the fritter when the edges turn brown.

    _____ Coat the skillet with cooking spray.

    _____ Peel the bananas.

    _____ Add the nutmeg to the syrup.

3. What will happen if you stir the pancake batter for too long?

    _____

    _____

4. Explain how pancakes and banana akara are similar and different.

    _____

    _____

    _____

5. The three tips at the beginning of the selection are all related to

    _____ safety.   _____ choosing ingredients.   _____ cooking for a crowd.

6. Why do you think the bananas in the banana akara recipe need to be very ripe?

    _____

7. What is your favorite special breakfast? List as many ingredients in it as you can.

    _____

    _____

    _____

Ready for a New Friend

Will Estéban want to get a new dog?

1   "I'm home, Mom!" called Estéban as he tossed his backpack on the bench in the hallway. "Are we still going to the mall to buy my shoes tonight?"

2   "I almost forgot," said Mrs. Ramirez, giving Estéban a quick kiss on the top of his head. "Things were a bit chaotic at work this afternoon."

3   "No problem," Estéban replied. "Can we still go to the mall, though?"

4   "Of course we can," said Mrs. Ramirez, hunting for her keys in her purse.

5   Estéban and Mrs. Ramirez were both surprised at how quickly they found the pair of shoes Estéban was looking for. As they left the athletic store, they passed a couple walking in the opposite direction. The man walked slowly, and he gripped the leash of a red harness in his hand. At the other end of the leash was a chocolate Labrador with glossy fur and an eager, friendly face.

6   "Mom," said Estéban as they walked to the parking lot, "was that a seeing-eye dog?"

7   "Yes," replied Mrs. Ramirez. "He looked like such a good, attentive dog, didn't he?" she asked her son, smiling.

8   "Sure," said Estéban. "Are they allowed to go anywhere?"

9   "I think they can go almost anywhere people can," said Mrs. Ramirez. "That's what the dogs are there for—to help their owners do everyday things that they might need a little extra help doing."

10   "I miss Sadie," said Estéban suddenly. Sadie was the sweet-natured mutt that the Ramirez family had adopted when Estéban was just a baby. She had died nearly six months ago, but Estéban still thought of her almost every day.

11   Mrs. Ramirez unlocked the car door and gave Estéban a quick hug with one arm. "I miss her, too, sweetie," she said. "That dog had such a good heart, didn't she?"

12   Estéban nodded. "Mom, you said to tell you when I thought I might be ready to get another dog."

13   Mrs. Ramirez smiled at Estéban in the rearview mirror. "I thought you might be ready soon. How do you feel about the idea of being a foster family to a puppy that will grow up to be a seeing-eye dog?" she asked.

14   Estéban was quiet for a moment. "We'd have to give the puppy back, though, wouldn't we?"

15   "Yes, we'd only have the puppy for about a year. It would be our job to socialize her so she would get used to lots of different kinds of people and places."

16   Estéban grinned. "I think we'd be the perfect foster family for a puppy," he said.

17   "Let's talk about it with your dad tonight," Mrs. Ramirez said. "Then, maybe we can find out some more information on the Internet."

18   "We're getting a puppy!" said Estéban to himself, leaning back in his seat. "There will be so much to teach her!"

1. Number the events below in the order in which they happened in the story.

_____ Mrs. Ramirez asked Estéban if he would be interested in fostering a puppy.

_____ Estéban said that he missed Sadie.

_____ Mrs. Ramirez looked for her keys in her purse.

_____ Estéban saw a man with a seeing-eye dog at the mall.

_____ Estéban and Mrs. Ramirez went to the mall.

2. Estéban and his mother went to the mall because _____.

3. Who is Sadie?

_____

_____

4. Why would the Ramirez family only have a foster puppy for about a year?

_____

_____

5. A **summary** is a short sentence that tells the most important facts about a topic. Check the sentence below that is the best summary for paragraph 5.

_____ The chocolate Labrador wore a red harness.

_____ On their way out of the store, Estéban and his mom passed a man walking a dog with a harness.

_____ Estéban found the shoes he wanted.

Write the words from the story that have the meanings below.

6. in a state of great confusion

_____
Par. 2

7. something that fits around an animal's upper body

_____
Par. 5

8. alert; giving a lot of attention to

_____
Par. 7

9. abruptly; all at once

_____
Par. 10

A Big Decision

What would it be like to foster a puppy?

1   On the first day of classes, the Ramirez family arrived early at the Seeing-Eye Dog Center. They were going to learn about being a foster family for a puppy.

2   "Okay, group," said Mr. Crockett. "I think we're ready to begin." He was a tall man with a graying beard. "How many of you are here tonight because you might like to foster one of our puppies?"

3   About half the people in the group raised their hands. Mr. Crockett nodded. "First of all, you should know how happy we are to have you here. Fostering a puppy is very important work. I think you'll find it very satisfying, but it is also quite demanding."

4   "What do you think some of your responsibilities will be?" Mr. Crockett asked.

5   Estéban raised his hand. "Well, I think it will be our job to make sure the puppy gets used to being around people. We'll have to take her to lots of different places, like shopping malls and ball games."

6   "That's right," said Mr. Crockett. "You should try to expose your puppy to things like crowds, the sounds of traffic, riding in cars or on buses, and other animals. That way she won't grow up to be a dog who gets frightened or startled easily."

7   A teenage girl with curly light brown hair sat across the room from Estéban. She rested one hand lightly on the back of a golden retriever who sat beside her chair. "This is Mitzi," she said, patting the dog on her side. "We've had her for about nine months. When you get your puppies, you have to be ready to spend a lot of time with them. They might feel lonely at first. Most of them have never been away from the other pups in the litter until they come to live with you. The first couple of nights we had Mitzi, I actually slept in a sleeping bag on the floor so I could be near her. It made her feel safe and comfortable."

8   The girl chuckled. "I don't recommend more than a couple of nights on the floor, though." She grinned and rubbed her back at the memory.

9   "What questions do you have so far?" asked Mr. Crockett as he looked around the circle.

10   "How can you give up the puppies after a whole year?" asked Estéban. "Don't they feel like part of your family by then?" This is what had worried him most about the idea of fostering.

11   Mr. Crockett nodded. "I can't tell you that it isn't hard," he said. "My family and I have fostered seven dogs over the years, and we loved every one of them. You just need to remember how important these dogs will be to their new companions. They really help open up the world to people who are blind. If you can remember what a gift seeing-eye dogs are, it becomes a little easier to say good-bye."

12   As the meeting ended, Mr. and Mrs. Ramirez turned to Estéban. "What do you think?" asked Mr. Ramirez. "Is this something we can handle? It will be a big responsibility."

13   Estéban looked at his dad. "I know we can do it, Dad. I can't wait to meet our puppy."

1. Puppies may feel lonely at first because
_____ .

2. Why does a foster family need to expose a puppy to lots of different things?

_____

_____

3. Why does Estéban feel worried about giving up a puppy after a year?

_____

_____

4. Do you think Mr. Crockett will foster more seeing-eye puppies in the future? Why or why not?

_____

_____

5. Check the words that describe Estéban.

_____ responsible

_____ kind

_____ competitive

_____ funny

_____ thoughtful

6. Write **F** before sentences that are facts. Write **O** before sentences that are opinions.

_____ About half the people at the meeting are thinking about fostering a puppy.

_____ Fostering puppies is an enjoyable way to spend time.

_____ Estéban and his parents will be a good foster family.

_____ The girl sitting across from Estéban has curly hair.

7. What is the setting for this story?

_____

8. What does Mr. Crockett say is helpful when saying good-bye to a foster dog?

_____

9. Would you be interested in fostering a guide dog? Why or why not?

_____

_____

Not Just Monkeying Around

Do you think that animals other than dogs can be trained to help people?

1 Have you ever heard of Monkey College? Who do you think goes to school there? If you said monkeys, you were right. Dogs are not the only animals that can be trained to help people. Helping Hands, an organization in Cambridge, Massachusetts, trains capuchin monkeys to be companions and helpers for people in wheelchairs who cannot move their arms or legs.

2 More than 20 years ago, Dr. M. J. Willard was working with a person who had recently become paralyzed. She thought that a monkey might be able to help her patient with some basic household chores. Dr. Willard was right. Not only can monkeys be trained to help people, they are also wonderful companions.

3 Capuchin monkeys are found in the wild in South Central America. They are about the size of a small cat and can live to be nearly 40 years old. They are very intelligent. They are also known for being friendly and good with their hands. Capuchin monkeys have opposable thumbs, which means they can use their hands much in the way that people do.

4 Everyday tasks, like turning on a light, putting something in the microwave, or pressing *play* on a CD player, can be difficult for someone who cannot use his or her arms and legs. Capuchin monkeys can easily perform these tasks. This allows their owners more freedom. They can accomplish things on their own and can live independently.

5 The monkeys and their owners become friends and learn to depend on each other. Some owners say the monkeys are almost like children to them. The monkeys can be mischievous and sometimes like to play tricks on their owners. This is especially true of young monkeys. Mostly, though, they like to please their owners. They like the treats they receive when they do a good job, and they like to be praised. Capuchin monkeys also love the affection they get from their companions. They love to snuggle, too.

6 Helping Hands matches people with disabilities to monkey companions who can help them. But the close friendships between the monkeys and their owners happen all on their own.

1. Check the sentence that best states the main idea of the story.

    _____ Monkeys are fun to have as pets.

    _____ Monkeys can be trained to help people with disabilities.

    _____ Monkeys can be mischievous.

2. Name two reasons why monkeys are good at helping humans.

    _____

    _____

3. Where is Helping Hands located?

    _____

4. Where do capuchin monkeys live in the wild?

    _____

Write **T** before the sentences that are true. Write **F** before the sentences that are false.

5. _____ Capuchin monkeys live to be about 20 years old.

6. _____ Capuchin monkeys can learn to perform many different tasks.

7. _____ Dr. Willard taught capuchin monkeys to speak.

8. _____ Most monkey owners form a strong relationship with their companions.

9. Why is it important that monkeys have opposable thumbs?

    _____

    _____

10. What kind of relationship do most companion monkeys and their owners have?

    _____ distant   _____ troubled   _____ close

11. What is the author's purpose for writing this selection?

    _____

    _____

    _____

Monkey Training

What would it be like to live with a monkey?

1   It is not that rare to hear of a family who is fostering a puppy for a seeing-eye dog school. It is much more unusual to hear of a family who is fostering a capuchin monkey for the Helping Hands organization.

2   Just like puppies, young monkeys need to be socialized before they can be trained as human helpers. One difference is that monkeys live longer than dogs do. This means that a monkey's "childhood" is also longer than a dog's. They need plenty of time to play and act like children before they are ready to settle down to the serious business of training. Monkeys may spend four to six years in a foster home before they are ready to begin training. The foster families say it is almost as much work as raising a young child!

3   Once a monkey begins training, it usually takes about a year for it to learn enough tasks to be a good helper. When a monkey is learning a task, it is rewarded with a treat. If the monkey makes a mistake, it is not punished; it just does not get a treat for that task.

4   One thing that the monkeys need to learn is how to follow commands. For example, if a person wants to have the lights turned on, he or she might give the command "sun." If the owner has dropped something, he or she might say "fetch." The monkey will know just what its owner means by these commands, and it will complete the task. Then, it will often get a reward like a pat on the head or a lick of peanut butter.

5   As the monkeys get better at completing their tasks, they learn new and more difficult ones. Some monkeys can scratch an itch on their owners or even learn how to use a computer!

I. Does a dog or a monkey have a longer "childhood"?

_____

2. Name two tasks the article says that a monkey can do for a person.

_____

_____

3. How long do monkeys spend in a foster home before they begin their training?

_____

4. Why do you think it is more common for people to foster dogs than monkeys?

_____

_____

5. Check the phrase that best describes the author's purpose.

_____ to compare different types of monkeys

_____ to share information about how companion monkeys are trained

_____ to convince the reader to get a monkey as a pet

6. Check the sentence below that is the best summary for paragraph 2.

_____ Monkeys have a longer life span than dogs.

_____ Monkeys need time to grow up before they can be socialized as human helpers.

Write the words from the article that have the meanings below.

7. taught how to behave correctly

_____
                              Par. 2

8. given something in return for a service or good behavior

_____
                              Par. 3

9. an order

_____
                              Par. 4

10. to finish

_____
                              Par. 4

Soccer Summer

Have you ever attended a sports camp?

1   "Eliza, have you decided what you'd like to do during the week that Mom and I will be in California this summer?" asked Eliza's dad. He and Eliza were setting the table for dinner.

2   "Well," said Eliza, "I'd rather go to California with you and Mom."

3   "I know, Eliza. We wish you could come with us, too. But it's just going to be so busy with all the meetings we have to go to that you wouldn't have any fun. Actually, I'd trade places with you in a second," said Dad with a big grin. "You don't think Mom would notice if I went to horseback riding camp or soccer camp, do you?" he joked.

4   Eliza laughed. "I'm pretty sure she'd notice, Dad. I guess that if I can't go with you and Mom, I'd like to go to soccer camp. Madeline is going, so at least I'll know someone, even if I'm not very quick on the field."

5   "Eliza, I think you'll do just fine," said Dad. "I know it's a little scary to go to a new place and meet so many new people. I think you'll be glad you did it, though," he said, resting his hand on her shoulder. "Besides, I've seen you play soccer. You're more talented than you think you are."

6   When Eliza and Madeline arrived at camp, they were happy to see that two girls from their class were also enrolled. "Now I feel a little more at home," said Eliza happily.

7   On the first day of camp, the counselors had the girls choose teams. Eliza was surprised that she was chosen as captain of her team, the Quick Kickers. That afternoon, the girls practiced several drills. Eliza was the first one done with each task the counselors assigned. She did her best to cheer on her teammates as they completed the course.

8   At the end of the first practice, a shy girl named Annie approached Eliza. "I just wanted to say thanks for helping us stay focused out there," said Annie. "I was really nervous about coming to camp, but you made me feel so comfortable and motivated."

9   Eliza couldn't help laughing. "Oh, Annie," she said, "I was probably even more nervous than you were!"

Circle the word that best completes each sentence and write it on the line.

1. Eliza finished each _____ the counselors assigned.

   task   conversation   team

2. Annie talked to Eliza after the first _____.

   lesson   practice   evening

3. Dad thinks Eliza is a _____ soccer player.

   funny   talented   lazy

Write **B** if the sentence describes something that happens before Eliza goes to camp.
Write **A** if the sentence describes something that happens after Eliza gets to camp.

4. _____ Madeline and Eliza are happy to see that two girls they know are enrolled.

5. _____ Eliza tells Annie she was nervous.

6. _____ Dad and Eliza set the table for dinner.

7. _____ Annie thanks Eliza for helping her stay focused.

8. _____ Dad tells Eliza that she'll do fine at camp.

9. Do you think Eliza will want to go to camp again next summer? Why or why not?

   _____

   _____

   _____

10. Why does Eliza tell Annie that she felt nervous?

    _____

    _____

    _____

11. Write about a time you tried something new that made you feel nervous at first.

    _____

    _____

    _____

Play Ball!

How did soccer become such a popular sport in the United States?

1   What if someone asked you to go to an association football game? Would you be interested? You might be more interested if you knew they were talking about soccer, the world's most widely played sport. Games similar to soccer were played as long as two thousand years ago in China! Modern soccer got its name from association football, a game played in England in the mid-1800s. The word *association* was shortened to *assoc*, which finally turned into *soccer*.

2   The first soccer clubs were formed in England in the 1850s. The first professional players joined in the 1880s. Soccer quickly spread across Europe and became very popular in countries such as Spain, Italy, and Germany. Soccer even spread to countries in faraway South America. People seemed to like how simple the game is. All you need to play are a ball and two goals. Everything else comes from the players. Soccer still remains incredibly popular in both Europe and South America. Professional players there are often as popular as movie stars are in the United States.

3   One of the best and most famous of these professionals is Edson Arantes do Nascimento. He is better known by his nickname, Pelé. Pelé was born in Brazil, a country in South America. With Pelé's help, Brazil won three World Cup titles from the late 1950s to the early 1970s. Today, he is still one of the all-time leading scorers in World Cup history with 12 goals. The International Olympic Committee named Pelé Soccer Player of the Century in 1999.

4   The World Cup is the worldwide soccer competition that is held every four years, once for women and once for men. More than 200 teams work hard to be chosen as one of the 32 best teams that get the honor of competing in the Men's World Cup. Millions of people worldwide watch the matches on television. The first Women's World Cup match was played in 1991 in China. Today, about 100 teams compete for just 16 spots.

5   It took longer for soccer to be accepted in the United States than it did in other places around the world. A different kind of football was already being played in this country. People were not eager to try another form. After Pelé joined the New York Cosmos in 1975, soccer became more popular in the United States. It continues to grow in popularity. Today, soccer is the second favorite sport for kids in the United States!

1. Number the events below in the order in which they happened in the selection.

   _____ Pelé was named Soccer Player of the Century.

   _____ The first soccer clubs were formed in England.

   _____ Games similar to soccer were played in China.

   _____ Pelé joined the New York Cosmos.

2. Check the reason the author probably wrote this story.

   _____ to tell people about the history and popularity of soccer

   _____ to explain how the game of soccer is played

   _____ to show how soccer got its name

3. Name two European countries where soccer is popular.

   _____

4. What do you need to play a game of soccer?

   _____

5. In what country was Pelé born?

   _____

6. It took longer for soccer to be accepted in the United States because

   _____

   _____.

7. How long ago were games similar to soccer first played in China?

   _____

8. The game that Americans call soccer is referred to as _____ in many other countries.

9. What is the World Cup?

   _____

10. Describe what you like or dislike about the game of soccer.

   _____

   _____

Quick Feet and a Big Heart

What is it like to play soccer professionally?

1   When Mia Hamm was growing up, there were not many female athletes to have as role models. Today, there are many more women in professional sports. Mia Hamm, often called the world's best all-around female soccer player, is happy to be a role model for many young athletes, both girls and boys.

2   Mariel Margaret Hamm was born in 1972 in Selma, Alabama. Her father was in the military, so she moved around a lot as a child. Mia's mother wanted her to take ballet lessons, but Mia was not interested. She wanted to take soccer lessons, instead. This turned out to be the right choice for her. Mia was just 15 years old when she became the youngest player ever to get a spot on the U. S. National Team!

3   Mia attended college at the University of North Carolina at Chapel Hill. She helped the women's soccer team there win the national championship four times in a row. When Mia graduated, her number was retired. This is a great honor for any athlete.

4   In 1991, the first Women's World Cup was held in China. At only 19 years old, Mia was the youngest member of the team, but she still helped the United States win the title.

5   In the 1996 Olympic Games in Atlanta, Georgia, Mia was proud to lead the women's team as it won a gold medal. More sports fans came to watch this game than had ever before attended a women's event. This was a good sign that women's sports were being taken more seriously in the United States. In 2004, Mia helped the U.S. team win another gold medal. She retired from the national team later that year, so the victory at the Athens Olympics was very meaningful for her.

6   During her career, Mia scored 158 goals in international competition. This made her a record-holder for goal scoring in international matches until 2013, when American Abby Wambach set a new record of 160 goals.

7   Since her retirement, Mia has had more time to devote to the charities that are important to her. In 1997, Mia's older brother Garrett died of a bone marrow disease. Mia and her brother had been very close. In his honor, Mia started the Mia Hamm Foundation to raise money to fight bone marrow disease and to support sports programs for girls. Mia also works with many other charities. She likes to help other young athletes, both boys and girls, achieve their goals.

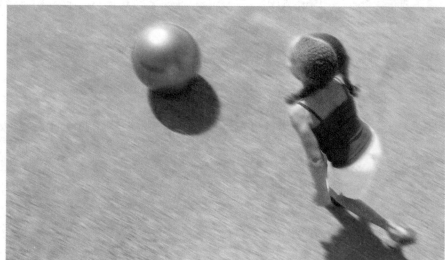

Write **T** before the sentences that are true. Write **F** before the sentences that are false.

1. _____ Mia Hamm was born in Chapel Hill.

2. _____ Mia's brother's name was Garrett.

3. _____ Mia is happy to be a role model for young athletes.

4. _____ Mia wanted to take ballet lessons when she was younger.

5. _____ Mia helped her team win a gold medal in the 1996 and 2004 Olympics.

6. Why did Mia start the Mia Hamm Foundation?

   _____

   _____

7. Explain why Mia might enjoy being a role model for girls.

   _____

   _____

8. Why do you think Mia Hamm has been so successful in her life?

   _____

   _____

9. Check the sentence that best states the main idea of the selection.

   _____ Mia Hamm liked playing soccer better than taking ballet lessons.

   _____ Mia Hamm is a talented athlete and a giving person.

   _____ Mia Hamm helped her college team win the national championship four times.

Write the words from the article that have the meanings below.

10. mark of excellence

    _____
    Par. 3

11. of two or more countries

    _____
    Par. 6

12. to help or to supply

    _____
    Par. 7

13. reach; accomplish

    _____
    Par. 7

Scoring a Goal

How has Mitch Arnold brought soccer to kids all over the world?

1   Many people wish they could make the world a better place. When Mitch Arnold was 13 years old, he found a way to do just that. A school principal from Haiti was visiting Mitch's church. He spoke about the poor children of Haiti. Mitch decided he wanted to help needy children around the world.

2   Mitch Arnold has always been an avid fan of soccer. He loves playing the game. He loves watching it. He loves talking about it. It made perfect sense that he would help give other kids a chance to enjoy the game he loves. Mitch came up with the idea for an organization called Peace Is The Goal. He earned money for his group by babysitting. He also worked as a referee for youth soccer games.

3   In 2011, Mitch won an amazing award. It is called the Gold M award, and it is given to young athletes who are role models in their communities. Along with the award came a check for $20,000! Mitch was delighted. That money could buy a lot of soccer balls!

4   Peace Is The Goal gives soccer equipment to poor kids. Mitch calls soccer "the world's game." People love it in almost every country of the world. He was sad to learn that many kids play soccer using things like rocks or plastic bottles as balls. He and his group began donating soccer balls, cleats, shin guards, and uniforms. He receives donations from other people, even kids, who want to help. Mitch also works with businesses to get the best deals he can on equipment. Then, he helps to pack it and ship it to places like orphanages, schools, churches, and missions.

5   Today, Mitch is a 21-year-old college student. He has donated over 4,000 pieces of soccer equipment to kids in more than 100 countries! Mitch's goal is to give kids something positive to do. He wants to spread a message of peace and hope. He wants kids to know that someone cares. And Mitch isn't satisfied yet. He wants to continue to help his organization grow. Nothing can stop this caring soccer player from reaching his goals.

1. What inspired Mitch to start Peace Is The Goal?

   _____

2. In paragraph 2, it says that Mitch is an avid fan of soccer. What does this mean? What clues in the text did you use?

   _____

   _____

3. Which words best describe Mitch Arnold?

   _____ stingy   _____ shy   _____ generous

   _____ athletic   _____ thoughtless _____ determined

4. Why does Mitch call soccer "the world's game"?

   _____

5. As a young teenager, how did Mitch earn money to support his organization?

   _____

6. Peace Is The Goal has donated soccer equipment to kids in more than _____ countries.

   _____ 40   _____ 60   _____ 100

7. Why do you think Mitch named his organization "Peace Is The Goal"?

   _____

   _____

8. *Now that Mitch is an adult, he no longer works with Peace Is The Goal.* Is this statement true or false?

   _____

9. What is the author's purpose in writing this selection?

   _____

10. If you could start your own charity, who or what would you want to help? Explain.

    _____

    _____

    _____

    _____

Applecreek Orchard

Have you ever picked fruit in an orchard?

1   On Friday morning, the sky was bright and clear, and the air was crisp. The school bus turned onto the gravel road that led to Tomás's uncle's apple orchard. As the bus pulled up to the small white house with green shutters, a large man with dark hair and a wide grin came outside.

2   Tomás's class got off the bus and stretched. Ms. Hallowell shook Uncle Luis's hand. "Thank you so much for allowing our class to visit your orchard," she said. "It's all they could talk about this week."

3   Uncle Luis laughed. "Well, I'm glad you could all come," he said to the class. "Are you ready to do some picking?" he asked in a booming voice.

4   "Yes!" shouted Ms. Hallowell's class.

5   "Well, hop up on the tractor bed, and remember to keep your arms and legs inside at all times," said Uncle Luis.

6   Tomás's uncle stopped the tractor at the beginning of a neat row of trees that were bursting with ripe fruit. He turned to the class. "Northern California is a wonderful place to grow apples," he said. "We have a lot of the weather they like—rainy springs, warm summers, and cool, crisp nights. Here at Applecreek Orchards, we mostly grow three varieties of apples: Granny Smith, Braeburn, and Pink Lady. Today, you'll be picking Braeburn apples. They are sweet, spicy, and crisp. They taste good raw, but they are also good for cooking."

7   "Who picks all your apples?" asked Cara, who was sitting next to Tomás.

8   "Every fall, I hire a crew to come and help me pick them. They work long days, seven days a week, just to make sure that the apples are picked at the right time," answered Uncle Luis.

9   "Once all the apples are picked, what do you do all winter?" asked Tomás's friend Kelly. "Do you get to go on vacation?"

10 Uncle Luis chuckled. "There is still a lot of work to do in the orchard during the winter. We have to grade, or assign categories, to the apples. Then, they have to be packed and shipped all around the country. We ship apples to places as far away as Florida. We also have to prune the trees. That helps them stay healthy and grow in the spring. It also lets more light reach the leaves and the apples."

11 "Whew!" said Tomás. "That sounds like a lot of work."

12 Uncle Luis nodded and handed Tomás a glossy red apple he had just picked. "Try this," he told his nephew. Tomás bit into the apple, and a bit of sweet juice ran down his chin. "What do you think?" asked Uncle Luis. "Is it worth all the hard work?"

13 Tomás's mouth was full of apple, so all he could do was nod and smile.

Circle the word that best completes each sentence, and write it on the line.

1. At the farm, the school bus turned onto the _____ driveway.

   smooth   concrete   gravel

2. Uncle Luis's farm is in Northern _____.

   Maine   California   Arkansas

3. Tomás is Ms. Hallowell's _____.

   teacher   student   parent

4. Check the phrase that best describes the author's purpose.

   _____ to convince the reader to buy apples only from California orchards

   _____ to explain how to buy and run your own orchard

   _____ to tell a story about a class trip to an orchard

5. Name two types of apples Uncle Luis grows at Applecreek Orchards.

   _____   _____

6. Do you think Uncle Luis will take a vacation next winter? Why or why not?

   _____

   _____

   _____

7. Which word best describes the students in Ms. Hallowell's class?

   _____ creative   _____ bored   _____ excited

8. Describe what kind of climate apple trees like.

   _____

   _____

9. Why do you think apples might need to be shipped to places like Florida?

   _____

10. Why do the apple trees need to be pruned?

   _____

To Market, to Market

What kinds of things can you find at a farmers' market?

1   "I'll see you in a couple of days!" called Tomás's mom through the car window. "If you bring some apples home with you on Sunday, I promise I'll make a pie." Tomás and his uncle waved and headed back to the house. Uncle Luis was going to start selling his apples at the local farmers' market. Tomás was spending the weekend with his uncle to help him set up the fruit stand.

2   "What's the first thing we need to do?" asked Tomás.

3   "Well, I thought we could load my truck with everything we'll need to bring with us tomorrow," answered Uncle Luis. "We'll have to leave pretty early in the morning. Your days often start before dawn when you are a farmer."

4   Tomás and Uncle Luis carried basket after basket of fresh, fragrant apples to the truck. They loaded the long folding tables and the yellow striped awning. Finally, Uncle Luis added the wooden sign that said *Applecreek Orchards*.

5   "Can you think of anything we're forgetting?" Uncle Luis asked his nephew.

6   Tomás thought for a moment. "Won't you need money to make change for your customers? Also, I think we need a scale to weigh the apples."

7   "You're absolutely right, Tomás," said Uncle Luis. "This is just why I wanted your help. I have a change box in the house, and it's all ready to go, but I would have completely forgotten about bringing a scale. Good thinking!"

8   The next morning, Tomás and Uncle Luis were on the road just as the sky was beginning to turn as pink as cotton candy. They hadn't had any breakfast yet, but Uncle Luis promised Tomás that there would be plenty of choices at the farmers' market.

9   As they pulled into the town's small downtown area, Tomás could see more than a dozen vendors setting up their stands. When the truck was unloaded, Uncle Luis gave Tomás a few dollars and asked him to buy some breakfast. A few minutes later, Tomás returned with warm cinnamon buns that were frosted with a thin layer of melting sugar. He handed the money back to his uncle.

10   Uncle Luis looked surprised. "These look too good to have been free," he said. "What happened?"

11   Tomás grinned. "They wanted to trade the cinnamon rolls for a few fresh apples. It sounded like a good deal to me."

12   Uncle Luis nodded his head. "Tomás, it looks like you and I are in business together!"

1. Why is Tomás spending the weekend with his uncle?

_____

_____

2. Do you think Tomás will help Uncle Luis again? Why or why not?

_____

_____

3. What does Tomás remind his uncle to bring to the farmers' market?

_____

_____

4. What does Tomás get for breakfast? What does he plan to exchange for his breakfast?

_____

_____

Write **T** before the phrases that describe Tomás and **L** before the phrases that describe Uncle Luis.

5. _____ forgot to load the scale into the truck
6. _____ traded apples for cinnamon buns
7. _____ said that your days often start before dawn when you are a farmer
8. _____ waved to his mom in the driveway

9. Which category best describes this story?

_____ science fiction   _____ realistic fiction   _____ biography

10. Find the simile (a comparison using *like* or *as*) in paragraph 8. Write it on the line below.

_____

_____

11. Why is Uncle Luis surprised when Tomás returns his money?

_____

_____

12. What does Uncle Luis mean when he says that your days often start before dawn when you are a farmer?

_____

Bees in the Trees

How do bees help apple farmers?

1   Have you ever seen an apple tree in bloom? If you have, you know that the blooms are a delicate, pale pink that slowly fades to white. They make the air smell as sweet as honey. There is a good reason for this. Apple trees need to attract bees, and a sweet odor is just the thing to do it.

2   Bees can be picky. They do not like to fly when it is below 60 degrees outside. They also do not like being out in weather that is windy or rainy. Apple farmers know that their apples depend on bees, so many purchase bees to release into their orchards every spring. They usually release about one hive of bees per acre of orchard.

3   When the weather is good, the bees get to work. The bee collects the nectar from the apple tree's flowers. As it does this, its wings brush against the pollen. When the bee flies to another flower to gather more nectar, it pollinates that flower. A bee might pollinate one type of apple blossom with the pollen from another type of apple tree. This means that a seed from a Red Delicious apple might not produce a Red Delicious tree.

4   How do owners of apple orchards get the types of trees they want? To produce a certain type of tree, apple farmers use a process called *grafting*. They take a twig, or *scion* (SIGH-un), from the parent tree and attach it to a small, young tree. The two will grow together as a single plant. The scion contains buds that will produce new twigs and leaves that are the same type as the parent tree. Because it is so easy to create new varieties of apples, nearly 7,500 different types exist around the world.

5   Growing apples was a popular hobby with some of the most famous Americans. Presidents George Washington and Thomas Jefferson were both apple growers. They even liked to trade wood from their apple trees so they could grow new varieties.

6   The next time you bite into a sweet, crisp apple, think about its long history in America and the work of the bees and the apple farmers who helped it along.

Write **T** before the sentences that are true. Write **F** before the sentences that are false.

1. _____ Most apple tree blossoms are pale yellow.

2. _____ The sweet smell of the flowers attracts bees.

3. _____ Bees do not like to be out in bad weather.

4. _____ A Red Delicious apple seed will always produce a Red Delicious tree.

5. _____ There are about 3,500 varieties of apples around the world.

6. Why do apple farmers purchase bees?

   _____

7. How do bees carry pollen from one flower to another?

   _____

8. What is the name of the process apple farmers use to produce the type of apple tree they want?

   _____

9. What is a scion?

   _____

10. Number the following steps in the order in which they occur.

    _____ The scent of the flowers attracts bees.

    _____ The bee carries the pollen to another flower.

    _____ The bee collects nectar from the flower.

    _____ The apple tree flowers.

Write the words from the article that have the meanings below.

11. loses brightness or color

    _____
                              Par. 1

12. to draw to itself; to interest

    _____
                              Par. 1

13. to let go

    _____
                              Par. 2

14. a sweet liquid found in flowers

    _____
                              Par. 3

An Apple a Day

What kinds of foods can you make using apples?

Before you begin:

- Never use the stove without an adult's supervision.

- Always remember to keep the handle of the pan turned in so you cannot accidentally bump into it.

Homemade Applesauce

4 medium apples
$\frac{1}{2}$ cup water
$\frac{1}{4}$ cup sugar

$\frac{1}{8}$ teaspoon cinnamon
$\frac{1}{8}$ teaspoon nutmeg

1. Here are some other things you will need: a measuring cup, teaspoon, peeler, cutting board, knife, pan, wooden spoon, and a fork or potato masher.

2. First, peel the apples. Have an adult help you slice them. (You can throw away the cores.) Then, cut the apple slices into small chunks.

3. Put the apple chunks in the pan with the water. Let them simmer over medium heat for 15 minutes. Then, stir in the sugar, cinnamon, and nutmeg.

4. When the applesauce cools, mash the chunks with a fork or a potato masher. Serve with graham crackers or a spoonful of whipped cream. Refrigerate any applesauce you do not eat.

Baked Apples

4 large apples
$\frac{1}{4}$ cup brown sugar, firmly packed
1 teaspoon cinnamon
1 teaspoon nutmeg

$\frac{1}{4}$ cup raisins
$\frac{1}{4}$ cup chopped pecans or walnuts
4 teaspoons butter
$\frac{1}{2}$ cup apple juice or cider

5. Here are some other things you will need: a measuring cup, teaspoon, peeler, apple corer, small bowl, aluminum foil, and a baking dish.

6. Preheat the oven to 400°F.

7. Peel the apples and core them. Try not to remove the whole core. Leave a little of the core at the bottom of the apple to hold the juices. Place the apples in the baking dish.

8. Combine the brown sugar, cinnamon, nutmeg, raisins, and nuts in a small bowl. Spoon one-fourth of the mixture into the hollow core of each apple. Top each apple with 1 teaspoon of butter.

9. Pour the apple cider or juice into the baking dish. Cover the dish with foil and bake for 25 to 30 minutes. Serve warm.

1. Number the directions below from **1** to **5** to show the order in which they are listed in the recipe for baked apples.

   _____ Cover the dish with foil.

   _____ Preheat the oven.

   _____ Top each apple with butter.

   _____ Peel the apples.

   _____ Spoon the mixture into the hollow core.

Circle the word that best completes each sentence, and write it on the line.

2. You should _____ any applesauce you do not eat.

   forget   refrigerate   donate

3. Use a wooden spoon to _____ in the sugar.

   whip   squeeze   stir

4. Spoon part of the _____ into the hollow core.

   mixture   apple   cider

5. Why shouldn't you remove the whole core when you make baked apples?

   _____

   _____

6. How many ingredients do you need to make baked apples?

   _____

   _____

7. How long do you need to bake the apples?

   _____

   _____

8. You can use a fork or a _____ to mash the apples.

9. How does the recipe suggest you serve the applesauce?

   _____

10. What is your favorite apple dish? If you've cooked with apples before, tell about your experience.

    _____

    _____

    _____

A New Virginia Home

Have you ever gone hiking?

1   It was the first weekend that Amira and her family had spent in their new house. Amira had finished unpacking the boxes in her bedroom. On one wall of her room, she hung a map of Michigan. That was the state her family used to live in. She would miss going to visit Lake Michigan and all the fun she'd had at the beach. On another wall, Amira hung a map of Virginia, the state that was her new home.

2   Amira heard a soft tapping. She saw her father's head poke around the door. "Hi, Dad," said Amira. "What's going on?"

3   "I just wanted to see how you were doing," said Dad. "Your room is starting to look pretty good. I like the maps."

4   "Thanks," said Amira, sighing and flopping down on the bed.

5   Dad sat next to her. "Why the big sigh?" he asked.

6   "I guess I miss Michigan and my friends," said Amira. "I don't know anyone here, and there's nothing to do."

7   "There are some kids your age who live on this block, but they may be on vacation still," said Dad. "I know you'll meet people as soon as school starts next week. As far as there being nothing to do, you're in luck. I'm looking for someone to go hiking with me this afternoon." Amira's dad stood up and walked over to the map of Virginia.

8   "We were lucky to move near one of the greatest hikes in the country," he said. "Have you ever heard of the Appalachian Trail?" he asked, tracing something on the map with one finger. Amira shook her head.

9   "Well, then, I think you ought to put on your hiking boots, grab some bug spray, and come along with me," said Dad.

10   Amira sighed again, but she looked a little bit interested. "I'm pretty sure you won't regret it," said Dad. "I'll meet you downstairs in 15 minutes, okay?"

11   Amira nodded and walked to her closet to look for her hiking boots. Fifteen minutes later, Amira and her dad said good-bye to her mom and drove to the trailhead. In her backpack, Amira carried some bug spray, a water bottle, two granola bars, and two oranges. In Dad's backpack, there was a cell phone, a water bottle, a tree identification guide, sunscreen, and a camera.

12   As Amira and her dad hiked through the woods, she felt her spirits start to lift. The air smelled clean and fresh, and a slight breeze whispered through the treetops. When Dad turned around, he noticed a big grin on Amira's face.

13   "That's nice to see for a change," joked Dad.

14   "This is great," she answered. "I don't miss Michigan nearly so much right now."

1. Check the reason the author probably wrote this story.

    _____ to tell a story about a girl and her dad and a hike they went on

    _____ to persuade the reader to hike the Appalachian Trail

    _____ to tell the reader facts about the Appalachian Trail

2. Check the sentence below that is the best summary for paragraph 7.

    _____ Amira's dad tries to make her feel better about the move to Virginia.

    _____ Amira's dad walked over to the map of Virginia.

3. Do you think Amira will want to go hiking again? Why or why not?

    _____

    _____

4. Name three things that can be found in Amira's backpack or her dad's backpack.

    _____

    _____

5. Check the words that you think best describe Amira's dad.

    _____ athletic

    _____ cheerful

    _____ angry

    _____ shy

    _____ caring

6. Why did hiking make Amira feel better?

    _____

    _____

7. What time of year is it? How do you know?

    _____

8. Choose one piece of dialogue from the story, and write it on the line. Tell what the dialogue tells you about the character or the story.

    _____

    _____

9. If you were trying to cheer up Amira, what would you do or say?

    _____

    _____

A Long Way Home

What are some hiking trails that are near your home?

1   What is the farthest you have ever walked? Was it to a friend's house on another block or to the store in your neighborhood? Imagine walking more than two thousand miles. The Appalachian Trail stretches from Georgia to Maine. It is one long hike, but thousands of people have walked the entire trail. Three to four million people use at least part of the trail every year for much shorter hikes.

2   In the 1920s, a man named Benton MacKaye thought that people who lived in cities would like to have a place where they could spend time in nature. This idea was the start of the Appalachian Trail. The first section opened in 1923 in Bear Mountain State Park, New York. In 1925, MacKaye went to Washington, D.C. to promote his idea. The Appalachian Trail Conference, or ATC, became the organization that would design and run the trail.

3   Myron Avery was one of the most important people involved in developing the trail. During the late 1920s, he spent all of his free time discovering and mapping almost the whole trail. He also encouraged many people to help him. By 1937, the trail had grown to 2,049 miles and ran from Springer Mountain, Georgia, to Mt. Katahdin, Maine, without any gaps.

4   However, right away the trail ran into some problems. In 1938, a hurricane destroyed a large section in New England that took many years to repair. An even bigger problem was traffic. Many people wanted to drive through the countryside and forests instead of hiking. The government decided that parts of the trail would be made into scenic roads. The Appalachian Trail had to be moved.

5   While the trail was being repaired and adjusted, the first "thru-hike," a hike of the whole trail from Georgia to Maine, was completed by Earl Shaffer in 1948. This hike was covered by the news. Many more people learned of the Appalachian Trail from the reports. Shaffer hiked the whole trail again in 1965, going from Maine to Georgia this time. Then, in 1998 at the age of 79, he did it again! He became the oldest person to thru-hike.

6   Because it takes about six months to hike the trail, people cannot carry all the food and other supplies they need. To solve this problem, hikers have their friends or family mail packages to towns along the route. Hiking the whole trail is not easy. Even though almost 2,500 hikers try to do it each year, only about 450 complete it. With good reason, thru-hikers are very proud of their accomplishment.

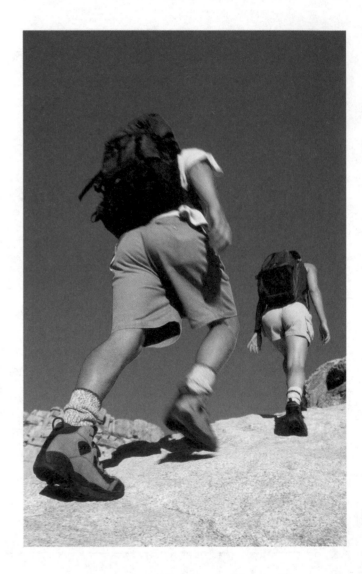

1. Where did the first section of the Appalachian Trail open?

   _____

2. Why can't people carry all the supplies they need with them on the trail?

   _____

3. About how many people hike the entire trail each year?

   _____

Write **T** before the sentences that are true. Write **F** before the sentences that are false.

4. _____ The Appalachian Trail goes from Georgia to Ohio.

5. _____ In the 1920s, Myron Avery mapped almost the whole trail.

6. _____ Part of the original Appalachian Trail had to be moved.

7. Check the sentence that best states the main idea of the selection.

   _____ It takes about six months to hike the entire Appalachian Trail.

   _____ The Appalachian Trail, built as a natural escape from city life, is the longest trail in the country.

   _____ The Appalachian Trail stretches from Springer Mountain, Georgia, to Mt. Katahdin, Maine.

8. Write **C** next to the sentence below that is the cause. Write **E** next to the sentence that is the effect.

   _____ Parts of the trail would be made into scenic roads.

   _____ Many people wanted to drive through the countryside and forests instead of hiking.

9. What is a thru-hike?

   _____

A **time line** shows the order in which things happened. Use the time line below to answer the questions that follow.

10. What happened in 1925?

    _____

11. When did a hurricane destroy part of the trail?

    _____

12. How many years after the hurricane did Shaffer complete the first thru-hike?

    _____

The Wild Side of the Trail

What kinds of wild animals do you see near your home?

1   If you ever decide to hike the Appalachian Trail, you might run into some interesting animals along the way. Hikers are often both excited and apprehensive about spotting a black bear. In some parts of the country, such as Georgia and the Great Smoky Mountains National Park, black bears have become used to humans and are no longer frightened of them. It might seem strange to you that a bear would be frightened of a human being. This fear often protects both bears and humans.

2   Most hikers do not run into a problem with bears on the trail. They just have to be sure to hang their food high in a tree at night. They also must be careful never to come between a mother bear and her cubs. A mother bear who thinks her cubs are in danger can be very aggressive.

3   Another type of animal that you might see if you hike the Appalachian Trail is a snake. There are many different kinds of snakes that live along the trail. Most of them are not poisonous, but there are poisonous copperheads and rattlesnakes in some areas. The best way to be safe around snakes is to wear boots for protection and to avoid putting your hands or feet in places you cannot see. It is also helpful to have a book that allows you to identify the animals you see.

4   The nine-banded armadillo might be one of the strangest and most unusual looking animals you could meet on the trail. The armadillo is a mammal whose name means *little man in armor* in Spanish. It has hard, bony plates that cover its head, body, and tail. Even though it is so well protected, the armadillo can also run quickly and burrow underground. It can even swim if it has to.

5   Another strange and interesting animal is the southern flying squirrel. This type of squirrel has an extra fold of skin between its front and rear legs. The skin acts as a sail or a parachute. Even though this squirrel cannot really fly, it can glide as far as 80 yards through the air, usually to get from one treetop to another.

6   If you walk quietly and look carefully, you might have a chance to see some animals that very few people ever have the opportunity to see in the wild.

1. Why do you think a hiker might be both excited and apprehensive about seeing a bear?

_____

_____

2. Why is it bad to come between a mother bear and her cubs?

_____

_____

3. What are two types of poisonous snakes you might see along the trail?

_____   _____

4. What does the name *armadillo* mean in Spanish?

_____

_____

5. Check the sentence below that is the best summary for paragraph 4.

_____ The armadillo can swim if it has to.

_____ The armadillo is a strange-looking animal that has many ways to protect itself.

6. Why do hikers have to hang their food high in a tree at night?

_____

7. What are the best ways to protect yourself against snakes?

_____

_____

8. What does the author say about animals in the conclusion of the article?

_____

_____

9. If you hiked the trail, what animal would you most like to see? Why?

_____

_____

_____

A Friendly Hike

Will Sarah and Edie accomplish their goal?

1   In March of 1999, Edie and Sarah began hiking the Appalachian Trail in Georgia. Sarah was a teacher, so she and Edie thought their hike would be an interesting learning experience for students. Before they departed, they visited classrooms for two weeks. Students had the opportunity to try on a backpack to see how much weight Sarah and Edie would be carrying during the trip. Students also were able to ask Sarah and Edie questions about the trail and doing a thru-hike. Sarah and Edie planned to post photos and journal entries on the Internet during the trip so that the students would be able to check on their progress.

2   Before they left, Sarah and Edie packed 18 boxes with supplies like crackers, granola bars, pasta, peanut butter, and dried fruits and vegetables. Their parents would mail the boxes to small towns along the trail so Sarah and Edie could pick them up along the way. That way, Sarah and Edie did not have to carry all their supplies with them from the beginning of the trip. Those backpacks would have been too heavy to lift.

3   Sarah and Edie met plenty of friendly hikers during their trip. People who are hiking the Appalachian Trail, or AT, often create "trail names" for themselves and their friends. That explains why Sarah and Edie met hikers with names like "Chewy" and "Baked Bean"!

4   There are many shelters along the AT. Hikers can stay there overnight, especially in times of bad weather. There are also books called *registers* at many of the shelters. Hikers can sign the books and leave notes for friends they have made who are also hiking the trail.

5   Sarah and Edie encountered all kinds of weather on their hike. They had days of beautiful clear weather, but they also hiked through rainstorms and thunderstorms. Once, they even saw thunder and lightning during a blizzard. Sometimes they hit icy spots along the trail, and sometimes the weather was so hot that they had to drink a lot of water. They did not want to become dehydrated.

6   When Sarah and Edie were in Virginia, there was a forest fire. They had to wait until it was completely out before the forest service would allow them to go back on the trail. Because of a fire in Shenandoah National Forest, they missed a 45-mile portion of the hike. Later in their trip, Sarah and Edie had someone drive them back there so that they would not miss a single mile of the AT!

7   Four and a half months after they began the hike in Georgia, Sarah and Edie completed it at Mt. Katahdin in Maine. They were close friends when they began their journey and even closer when they came home. They had accomplished their goal!

1. Why did Sarah and Edie plan to post journal entries and photos?

   _____

   _____

2. Do you think Sarah and Edie would recommend this hike to their friends? Why or why not?

   _____

   _____

3. Do you think Sarah and Edie will go hiking together again? Why or why not?

   _____

   _____

4. How long did it take Sarah and Edie to complete their hike?

   _____

Check the word that best completes each sentence.

5. Sarah and Edie thought their trip could be a(n) _____ experience for students.

   _____ educational   _____ normal   _____ boring

6. Sarah and Edie were _____ for the help of their families and friends.

   _____ annoyed   _____ entertained   _____ grateful

7. Bad weather is one _____ of the trip that hikers have to plan for.

   _____ type   _____ element   _____ shelter

8. Write one cause from the story and its effect.

   Cause: _____

   Effect: _____

9. Check the character traits that you think would be important for hikers on the Appalachian Trail.

   _____ athletic   _____ shy   _____ weak

   _____ good-natured   _____ knowledgeable   _____ irritable

10. Why did Sarah and Edie originally miss a portion of the trail? Why did they go back and hike it later?

    _____

    _____

On the Right Track

Where could you look for animal tracks?

1   The more time Amira and Dad spent hiking the Appalachian Trail, the more Amira enjoyed living in Virginia. She and Dad had seen squirrels, chipmunks, and many types of birds on their hikes. Amira kept seeing animal tracks, but she didn't know how to identify them.

2   "Why don't we bring Mom's digital camera with us on our next hike?" suggested Dad. "Then, we can take some pictures of the tracks we've seen. When we get home, we'll go to the library and see if we can find a book that has pictures of animal tracks."

3   "That's a great idea, Dad!" said Amira excitedly. "Do you think we might find some bear tracks?" she asked.

4   Dad raised his eyebrows. "I don't think I want to get that close to a bear," he said. "Actually, you and I probably don't hike far enough into the woods to see one."

5   "Well, I still hope we find some bear tracks," said Amira.

6   That weekend, Dad and Amira drove to a section of the Appalachian Trail that they hadn't hiked before. They brought lunch with them so they could spend the whole day in the woods. As soon as they got started, Amira spotted some tiny tracks in a muddy area near a tree. Dad showed her how to use the digital camera to take a close-up picture of the tracks.

7   "Good eyes!" he commented. "I think I would have walked right past those tracks."

8   As the day went on, Amira took pictures of more and more animal tracks. She seemed to see a new set every few minutes. By the end of the day, Amira was tired and dirty, but happy.

9   When they got home, Mom was excited to hear about their adventures. She knew that Dad and Amira were looking for tracks along the trail, so she had bought a small identification guide for them.

10   "This is great, Mom!" said Amira. She began flipping through the guide until she located pictures that looked like the ones she had taken that afternoon.

11   "Did you find any matches?" asked Mom.

12   "I found a lot of matches," answered Amira. "We took pictures of chipmunk, raccoon, deer, and skunk tracks."

13   "No bears?" asked Dad.

14   "Not yet," said Amira. "But I'm going to keep looking!"

NAME _____

1. Check the phrase that best describes the author's purpose.

_____ to explain where to look for bears on the Appalachian Trail

_____ to tell a story about the tracks a girl and her dad find while hiking

_____ to persuade the reader to take photos of animal tracks

2. Who do you think would rather see a bear—Amira or Dad? Why?

3. Name two types of tracks Dad and Amira found.

4. Why did Dad and Amira bring lunch with them?

5. How did Amira use the identification guide?

6. Why does Dad say, "Good eyes!" to Amira?

7. What activity has helped change how Amira feels about living in Virginia?

8. How is a digital camera useful in identifying animal tracks?

9. If you didn't have a camera, how else could you remember what the tracks look like?

10. Name several places where you might be able to look for animal tracks near where you live. What kinds of tracks do you think you might see?

Spectrum Reading Grade 4

53

A French Connection

Have you ever traveled to another country?

1   "I'd like to have everyone's attention, please," said Ms. Watkins. The fourth- and fifth-grade students at Robert Louis Stevenson Elementary School sat in the cafeteria for a special announcement after lunch. They weren't sure why the principal wanted to talk to them or why there wasn't an assembly for the whole school.

2   Ms. Watkins cleared her throat. "Your classmates Hannah and Jack are lucky enough to have the opportunity to live in France for the next year. Mr. DiSalvo will be teaching there, and his family will be joining him. I know Hannah and Jack will miss all of you. I'm sure that the year will go quickly, and they'll have all sorts of interesting stories to share with us when they return."

3   Hannah and Jack were sitting at the same table in the cafeteria. Hannah looked excited, but Jack looked a little nervous. "Hannah, Jack, do you have anything you'd like to add?" asked Ms. Watkins.

4   Hannah nodded. "We're going to do a lot of traveling while we're in France," she said. "My mom thought that the kids in our classes might want to write down any questions they have or anything they are curious about. We can look for the answers while we are there. Then, we can e-mail the answers to you at school."

5   Ms. Watkins smiled. "That is a marvelous idea!" she exclaimed. Then, she turned to the group. "I'd like everyone to think of a question or two for Jack and Hannah. They will be leaving in two weeks. Don't forget to give your questions to them and wish them *bon voyage*!"

6   Jack turned to his sister. "What does that mean?" he asked.

7   Hannah smiled. "That's what you say to people who are going on a trip. It's the French way of wishing someone happy, safe travels."

8   A moment later, Hannah's and Jack's classmates gathered around them. They had so many questions: "Are you going to go to the top of the Eiffel Tower?", "Will you know how to speak French when you get home?", "Where will you live?", "What kinds of foods do people eat in France?"

9   Jack and Hannah looked at each other and started to laugh. "I guess we'll have our work cut out for us, won't we?" said Hannah.

1. What does the phrase *bon voyage* mean?

_____

_____

2. Why will the DiSalvos be moving to France for a year?

_____

_____

3. Why do you think Jack feels nervous?

_____

_____

4. How will Jack and Hannah send answers to their classmates' questions?

_____

Write **T** before the sentences that are true. Write **F** before the sentences that are false.

5. _____ Hannah and Jack go to Robert Frost Elementary School.

6. _____ The DiSalvos are moving to France for two years.

7. _____ Jack doesn't know what *bon voyage* means.

8. _____ The students are gathered in the gym.

9. In paragraph 2, Ms. Watkins says that Hannah and Jack will have the opportunity to live in France. What does *opportunity* mean in this sentence?

_____

10. What is the setting for this story?

_____

11. Write two questions you would ask Hannah and Jack before their trip.

_____

_____

_____

Tower Power

Have you ever visited an important monument?

1 When someone mentions Paris, France, you might think of the Eiffel Tower. Do you know why it was built?

2 In the 1880s, the people of Paris were getting ready to celebrate the centennial of the French Revolution. This anniversary was going to occur in 1889, and the French wanted to build a special monument for this important day. A contest was held for the best design. More than seven hundred entries were received. The tower designed by Alexandre-Gustave Eiffel was immediately chosen as the best, and in 1887, construction was begun.

3 It took two years to build the Eiffel Tower. On March 31, 1889, the tower was finished and a flag was flown from the flagpole at the top. At 1,052 feet, it was the tallest building in the world, and it held that record until 1930. During its first year, two million visitors came to see the tower. Some of them climbed the 1,665 steps to get to the highest platform. A person standing at the top can see 42 miles away on a clear day!

4 It might seem as though something as large as the Eiffel Tower would be very solid. In fact, the tower moves all the time. On windy days, it sways by almost five inches! The tower's height also changes by as much as six inches, depending on the weather.

5 Although the Eiffel Tower is very popular today, it was almost torn down in 1909 because there were not as many people coming to see it. Luckily, the invention of the radio saved the tower. Because the tower was so tall, it was the perfect place to put an antenna for sending and receiving radio waves. When television came along, the tower was also used to transmit television programs.

6 Over the years, people have done some strange things at the Eiffel Tower. In 1954, a mountaineer climbed the outside of the tower. In 1984, two people parachuted from the top deck. Someone even rode a bicycle down hundreds of stairs from the first platform to the ground.

7 Today, the Eiffel Tower is as popular as ever. With almost seven million visitors a year, the Eiffel Tower has become the most well-known symbol of Paris.

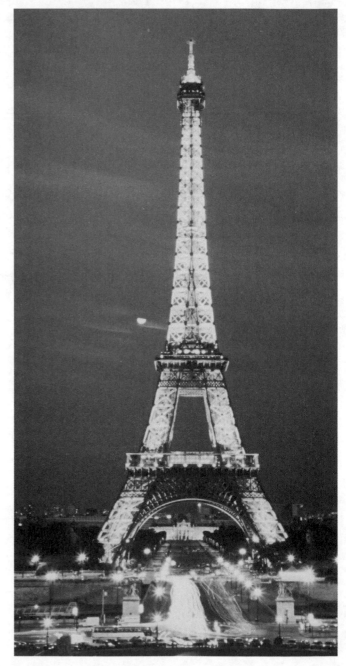

1. Number the events below from **1** to **5** to show the order in which they happened.

    _____ A mountaineer climbed the side of the tower.

    _____ The Eiffel Tower was almost torn down.

    _____ Alexandre-Gustave Eiffel's design was chosen.

    _____ Two people parachuted from the top deck of the tower.

    _____ France celebrated its centennial.

2. Why was the Eiffel Tower built?

    _____

    _____

3. How long did it take to build the Eiffel Tower?

    _____

    _____

4. How far does the tower sway on windy days?

    _____

5. Do you think the French will want to tear down the Eiffel Tower in the future? Why or why not?

    _____

    _____

6. What saved the Eiffel Tower in 1909?

    _____

    _____

Write the words from the article that have the meanings below.

7. marking the date of something that happened 100 years ago

    _____
    Par. 2

8. the date every year that marks a special event

    _____
    Par. 2

9. a statue or building that helps people remember something important

    _____
    Par. 2

10. a raised surface, like a stage

    _____
    Par. 3

Impressive Paintings

Is there an art museum in your town?

1   The DiSalvos were spending the morning at the Louvre, the famous museum in Paris. "I think that we need to decide what we want to focus on today," said Dad. "The museum might be a little overwhelming otherwise."

2   Mom agreed. "When I studied art history in college," she said, "the Impressionists were always my favorite. That is where I'd like to begin. How does everyone else feel about it?"

3   "The brochure says that the Impressionist paintings are in the Musée d'Orsay," said Hannah.

4   "That is a part of the Louvre," said Mom. "It's on the left bank of the river. Let's start over there, and then maybe we'll come back here after lunch."

5   Hannah and Jack were surprised at how many of the Impressionist paintings they recognized. "Don't we have a calendar of this artist at home?" Jack asked Mom.

6   "Yes," said Mom. "His name is Claude Monet. He's one of my favorite artists. I'm impressed that you recognized his paintings, Jack."

7   Jack grinned. "I always thought they were kind of boring," he admitted. "They're definitely more interesting in real life." Mom laughed and patted Jack on the shoulder as they walked into the next room.

8   "Look at this!" said Dad. "This painting is magnificent!"

9   "Shhhh!" said Mom and Jack at the same time.

10   "Dad, you're supposed to talk quietly in museums," Jack said to his father with a stern look.

11   "Where's Hannah?" asked Mom suddenly.

12   Mom, Dad, and Jack looked all around, but they couldn't find Hannah anywhere. "Maybe she's still in the last room," suggested Jack. They checked the last room they had visited, but there was no Hannah.

13   Then, Jack spotted his sister through the doorway of a room they hadn't visited yet. A group of French students wearing uniforms were standing in front of a painting and listening to a man talk.

14   Jack walked over to the group and tugged on his sister's hand. "Come on," he whispered. "Mom and Dad think you're lost!"

15   "Hannah, what on earth were you doing?" asked Mom, as Hannah and Jack joined their parents.

16   "I'm sorry," said Hannah. "There is a girl in that class who speaks English. Her name is Adrienne. She was telling me what her teacher was saying. Did you know that people in France used to think that the Impressionists were just bad artists?"

17   Mom and Dad hugged Hannah. "We're glad you made a friend and that you're enjoying the paintings here, but you had us really worried. We need to stick together," said Mom.

18   "We should have a meeting place in case we get separated again," added Dad.

19   "How about the café?" asked Jack.

20   Mom and Dad laughed. "Someone's ready for lunch!" said Mom.

1. Where are the Impressionist paintings located?

    _____

2. What is the name of one of Mom's favorite artists?

    _____

3. Why does Dad think the family should have a meeting place?

    _____

    _____

4. Do you think Hannah will want to come back to the Louvre on another day? Why or why not?

    _____

    _____

Write **H** on the line if the phrase describes Hannah. Write **J** if it describes Jack.

5. _____ recognizes Monet paintings from a calendar at home

6. _____ meets a French student named Adrienne

7. _____ tells Mom and Dad where the Impressionist paintings can be found

8. _____ suggests the café as a meeting place

Underline the word that best completes each sentence, and write it on the line.

9. Hannah and Jack _____ many of the Impressionist paintings.

    recognize   ignore   dislike

10. For a few minutes, Hannah _____ a group of French students.

    loses   joins   admires

An **idiom** is a group of words that has a special meaning. For example, the idiom *hit the hay* means *to go to bed*. Write the idiom from paragraph 17 on the line next to its meaning.

11. stay in a group; not get separated

    _____

12. Have you ever visited an art museum? If you have, tell about your visit. If you haven't, tell about what types of art you'd like to see.

    _____

    _____

    _____

A Museum Fit for a King

What museums have you visited?

1   Located on the Seine (SEN) River in the heart of Paris, the Louvre (LOOV) is the biggest art museum in the world. It has seven major areas, more than one hundred different rooms, and nearly 300,000 items in its collection. Even one whole day would not be enough to see the entire museum.

2   The Louvre is made up of several different buildings that were added over many centuries. The very first section, built more than eight hundred years ago, was originally used as a fortress to protect Paris from the Vikings. Within a hundred years, King Charles V had turned one of the towers into a library.

3   Even though it was used by French royalty to store their many possessions, it was not turned into a palace until the 1500s. During his reign, King Henry IV added a huge section called the Grande Galerie. This made the Louvre one of the biggest buildings in the world at that time. But the Louvre was not done growing yet! By 1624, King Louis XIII expanded it to almost four times the size it had been.

4   Meanwhile, the royal family continued to collect more and more art, which they kept at the Louvre. This art was only to be seen by the kings and queens and the people they might invite to view it. After the French Revolution, the art in the Louvre was available for everyone to enjoy. The museum opened to the public for the first time on November 8, 1793.

5   Today, the Louvre is owned and operated by the French government. French President François Mitterrand understood how important the Louvre was to the world. In 1981, he announced a massive project that would not only remodel the old parts of the museum, but also make the museum nearly twice as big as it already was!

6   Mitterrand also had the famous architect I. M. Pei (PAY) help solve a major problem. Because the museum was made up of so many buildings, visitors could not tell which door was the entrance. Pei's solution was to build a giant glass pyramid, which was based on the Louvre's Egyptian artifacts. The pyramid marks the entrance, and today everyone knows how to get inside.

7   Some of the most famous works of art ever created are on display at the Louvre. These include the *Mona Lisa*, painted by Leonardo da Vinci, as well as the sculptures *Winged Victory* and *Venus de Milo*. The museum also has important collections of artifacts from Islamic, Greek, and Roman history.

1. What is the name of the river on which the Louvre is located?

   _____

2. Do you think the Louvre will grow even larger in the future? Why or why not?

   _____

   _____

3. Who owns and operates the Louvre today?

   _____

4. Name one famous piece of art on display at the Louvre.

   _____

5. After what major historical event could the public see the art at the Louvre?

   _____

Write **B** if the sentence describes something that happened before the Louvre opened to the public. Write **A** if the sentence describes something that happened after the Louvre opened to the public.

6. _____ Mitterrand announced a project to expand the Louvre.

7. _____ The French Revolution began.

8. _____ One part of the Louvre protected Paris from the Vikings.

9. _____ I. M. Pei built a glass pyramid for the entrance.

10. _____ The Louvre was turned into a palace.

11. Look at the words *Seine* and *Louvre* in the first paragraph. Why is each of these words followed by a word in parentheses?

    _____

    _____

12. I.M. Pei built a glass pyramid to serve as an entrance to the Louvre. What problem did this solve?

    _____

    _____

13. How does the photo on page 60 add to your understanding of the article?

    _____

    _____

Seeing the World Through Different Eyes

What types of artwork do you like?

1   Today, artists can make whatever kind of art they want. A painting might be as realistic as a photograph, or it might look like smears and splashes across the canvas. Not very long ago, however, a powerful government organization in France decided what could and could not be be considered art. A brave group of painters, called the *Impressionists*, challenged these ideas and changed art forever.

2   In the middle of the 1800s, France was considered the most important place in the world for art. One reason for that was the Academy, a government organization with a strict set of rules about art. To be accepted by the Academy, an artist had to be very talented. Artists also had to paint exactly the way the Academy wanted them to. How could an artist be creative if he or she was told what to create?

3   Each year, the Academy had an exhibition of the art they had decided was the best. In 1864, a group of artists who did not get into the show became frustrated. They felt that their paintings were not bad; the paintings were just different. After complaining to the government, these artists were given their own show. It was called the *Salon des Refusés*, which means the *exhibition of rejects*.

4   The Academy thought all art should look realistic. The Impressionists wanted to explore other ideas. They were more interested in trying to show movement and the bright colors of daylight. For example, if you move your hand quickly in front of your face, it looks blurry. To the Impressionists, it was more real to show these blurry images than it was to paint a scene frozen like a photograph. It was also more interesting to show all of the different colors that occur when light hits an object like water.

5   By 1874, many different artists were painting in this new style, including Claude Monet. One of his paintings was titled *Impression: Sunrise*. A critic named Louis Leroy did not like these new artists. He thought their paintings looked unfinished. He used Monet's title to make fun of these painters by calling them "impressionists," meaning that they did not make real paintings, just sketches. The critics who liked these artists thought the word was just right. They began to use it in a positive way.

6   Some of the other Impressionists were Pierre-Auguste Renoir, Alfred Sisley, Edgar Degas, and Mary Cassatt. They thought it was more important to paint *how* they saw things, instead of just *what* they saw. Other artists around the world felt that they could have this freedom as well. Because of the Impressionists, the art world was never the same.

Regatta at Argenteuil by Claude Monet

The Cliff Walk at Pourville by Claude Monet

1. What was the Academy?

   _____

   _____

2. Why didn't Louis Leroy like the paintings of the Impressionists?

   _____

   _____

3. Name two Impressionists other than Claude Monet.

   _____

   _____

4. Which came first—frustrated artists were given their own show by the Academy, or Louis Leroy came up with the name *Impressionists*?

   _____

   _____

Write **F** before the sentences that are facts. Write **O** before the sentences that are opinions.

5. _____ The Impressionists challenged ideas about art.

6. _____ It is not fair that artists couldn't create the art they wanted to create.

7. _____ The Impressionists wanted to show movement and light in their paintings.

8. _____ The paintings of the Impressionists look unfinished.

9. _____ Artists should be allowed to have the freedom they need to be creative.

10. Check the sentence that is the best summary for paragraph 4.

    _____ The Impressionists did not think that paintings that looked like photographs were very interesting.

    _____ Instead of painting realistically, the Impressionists wanted to explore light and movement.

    _____ According to the Academy, all art should look realistic.

An E-mail from Overseas

*Have you ever written an e-mail or
received one from abroad?*

From: Hannah and Jack DiSalvo

Date: September 22, 2014

To: 4th and 5th graders at R.L.S. Elementary

Subject: Bonjour!

Bonjour! (That means *hello* in French.)

1   We hope you all had a great summer. Ours was a lot of fun. We have seen so many new things and met so many wonderful people. The French are very friendly. They have helped us adjust to living here and have made us feel welcome. There are so many things we want to share with all of you. We are going to have to send more than one e-mail, but here are our favorite highlights of our time in France so far. We are also including a few photos so you can see where we have been.

2   The best part of the summer was getting to see the Tour de France. It is the most famous bicycle race in the world. It is held every July. The riders travel more than two thousand miles over about a month! We got a quick glimpse of the riders as they sped past! After the race, our family rented bikes, and we rode along part of the route that the cyclists used. Here is a picture of us on our bikes in the heart of Paris.

3   A few of you asked whether the French really eat snails. The answer is yes. We went out to dinner a few weeks ago, and our parents ordered them. We each tried one, and it didn't taste too bad. The snails, called *escargots*, are served with lots of melted butter. They feel a little rubbery when you bite into them, but they don't actually have much taste. Jack's favorite food here is the French pastries. Hannah loves the fresh bread from the bakery down the street. Here is a picture of Jack eating a huge chocolate croissant.

4   We went to visit the Eiffel Tower a few weeks ago. We went all the way to the top. It was a sunny day, so we could see for miles and miles into the distance. Dad doesn't like heights, so he stayed at the bottom of the tower and took pictures from the ground.

5   We miss all of you a lot. Write back to us, and let us know what is new at home.

Au revoir! (Can you guess what that means in French?)

Hannah and Jack DiSalvo

1. What French word do Hannah and Jack use in the greeting of their e-mail?

   _____

2. What is the Tour de France?

   _____

   _____

3. Do you think Hannah and Jack will try more unfamiliar foods while they are in France? Why or why not?

   _____

   _____

4. Why didn't Mr. DiSalvo go to the top of the Eiffel Tower with his family?

   _____

5. Check the phrase that best describes the author's purpose.

   _____ to persuade the reader to try *escargots*

   _____ to tell a story about a family's experiences in France

   _____ to convince the reader to take a trip to Paris

Circle the word that best completes each sentence, and write it on the line.

6. You can see far into the _____ from the top of the Eiffel Tower.

   height   miles   distance

7. Without the butter, the *escargots* would be mostly _____.

   tasteless   rubbery   cooked

8. The French have made the DiSalvos feel _____.

   ignored   welcome   friendly

9. In paragraph 5, what does *au revoir* mean? How do you know?

   _____

   _____

10. How would you describe Jack and Hannah's experience in France so far?

    _____ lonely   _____ interesting   _____ dangerous

11. After reading this e-mail, do you think you would want to visit France? Why or why not?

    _____

    _____

Racing for the Yellow Jersey

What is the farthest you have ever ridden a bicycle?

1   Racing along country roads and through the cities of France each year, the best bicyclists in the world take part in the Tour de France. Not only is this contest one of the oldest and most popular sporting events on Earth, it is also one of the most difficult. Even though approximately 150 cyclists start each race, only about half reach the finish. That is not hard to believe when you learn that the Tour de France is nearly two thousand miles long and takes three weeks to complete!

2   In 1903, the race was held for the first time as a publicity event for the newspaper *L'Auto*. It was an instant success. Every July since then, the race has taken place. Only war has been able to interrupt the annual Tour de France. The race was not held from 1915 until 1918 because of World War I and from 1940 to 1946 because of World War II.

3   The Tour de France is divided into different races for each day, called *stages,* so that the racers do not have to ride all night. These stages also allow the race to take place all over France and sometimes in other countries. In 1988, the race's first stage actually took place in Ireland. The competitors then traveled to France to continue the rest of the race.

4   Each stage is also a different style of bicycle racing. Sometimes the terrain is flat, so the race is a sprint. At other times, the race goes through the mountains, so the bicyclist needs to have better endurance. Judges give points to the winner of each stage. The racer who is winning the most sprints gets to wear a green jersey. The winner of the most mountain races wears a white jersey with red polka dots.

5   The most important jersey is for the bicyclist who is in the lead. The racer who is finishing the stages the fastest is considered the leader. This rider gets to wear a yellow jersey. At the end of the race, the yellow jersey is awarded to the winner as a trophy.

6   For the last stage of the race, the cyclists sprint to the finish line along the famous Champs-Élysées (shawns ell-ee-ZAY), a cobblestone street in downtown Paris.

7   Until the 1980s, all of the winners were from Europe. Most were from France. In 1986, American Greg LeMond became the first bicyclist who was not European to win the Tour de France. He won again in 1989 in the closest finish of all time— only eight seconds ahead of the next racer! LeMond is not the only one to win the Tour de France more than once. Four riders have actually won the race five times each!

1. Check the phrase that best describes the author's purpose.

    _____ to explain why the Tour de France is the most interesting race in Europe

    _____ to share some facts about the Tour de France

    _____ to entertain the reader with funny stories about cyclists

2. Check the sentence that best states the main idea of the selection.

    _____ The Tour de France is the most difficult and popular bicycle race in the world.

    _____ The Tour de France includes different stages so the riders do not have to bike all night.

    _____ The racers may get to wear different colored jerseys throughout the race.

3. How many cyclists begin the race?

    _____

4. Why is the yellow jersey the most important?

    _____

5. Who was the first American cyclist to win the Tour de France?

    _____

6. What are two historical events that have interrupted the Tour de France?

    _____

7. In paragraph 4, the author says that sometimes the terrain is flat. What does *terrain* mean?

    _____

8. The winner of each stage gets to wear a special _____.

9. Why do you think that only about half the cyclists who start the race make it to the finish?

    _____

    _____

10. Name three qualities that you think a cyclist would need to complete the Tour de France.

    _____

    _____

Eat to Compete

What kinds of foods do riders in the Tour de France eat during the race?

1   Imagine going for a long bike ride. Maybe you've taken a daylong hike in the woods. Or, perhaps you have spent the afternoon playing basketball. What does your body need to keep going? Fuel! For the riders of the Tour de France, where and what they eat is important. The racers travel about 2,000 miles in three weeks. They even ride through the mountain chains of the Pyrenees and the Alps. Each day, the racers ride one stage of the race. Before, during, and after, they need energy to help them compete.

2   An average adult male needs about 2,500 to 3,000 calories a day. The racers, though, burn a huge number of calories each day. In fact, they can burn up to 4,500 calories just riding one stage. Racers need food that gives them immediate energy. They also need long-lasting energy. It's important that they eat foods they like and that are familiar. The last thing a rider needs on the Tour de France is an upset stomach!

3   Breakfast for the riders often includes foods like cereal, oatmeal, rice, and pasta. These are high carbohydrate foods. They give the athletes energy. They are also needed for muscle function. Just before the stage starts, riders often drink a mix that is high in carbs. Snacks like rice bars, power bars, and even sandwiches get the athletes through a stage.

4   As important as food is, making sure that racers drink enough is also important. You probably already know that when you exercise, you sweat. Racers need to drink liquids to stay hydrated. Drinking too much can be a problem, though. Even a little extra weight means more work for the racer. It can also make a racer slower. It's hard to get the right balance!

5   After a stage is over, racers refuel with water, energy drinks, and protein snacks. Protein can help repair muscles that are sore and tired. Finally, it's time for dinner. The last meal of the day is usually high in calories. It can have more calories than an average person eats in a day! Dinners are a mix of carbs, proteins, and fats. Vegetables add vitamins that help the body heal and recharge. The next day, the racers wake up. They yawn and stretch. Then, they get to work, fueling their bodies the day's competition.

1. Which of the following foods is likely to be high in carbohydrates?

_____ spaghetti   _____ lettuce   _____ a steak

2. Read the sentences below. Write **F** next to sentences that are facts and **O** next to sentences that are opinions.

_____ Meat, eggs, and beans are high in protein.

_____ Eating rice and noodles for breakfast is unpleasant.

_____ Energy drinks are more satisfying than water after racing.

3. Why do riders have to be careful about drinking too much liquid during a race?

_____

_____

4. Which meal of the day is usually highest in calories for racers?

_____

5. How does your body lose water when you exercise?

_____

6. Why is it important for riders to eat familiar foods and foods they enjoy?

_____

_____

7. In paragraph 2, it says that racers need food that gives them immediate energy. What does *immediate* mean?

_____

8. Describe an activity that you need extra energy to do. Do you eat differently when you do this activity?

_____

_____

_____

The Peregrine Project

Have you ever gone to an Earth Day celebration? What was it like?

1   On April 22, Akiko and Ben's elementary school was going to have an Earth Day celebration. There would be a table that would teach students about recycling. There would be sign-up sheets for clubs that clean up litter around town. There would be games with Earth-friendly prizes. Of course, there would also be all sorts of healthful foods and snacks. Akiko and Ben wanted to contribute something really special.

2   "It just seems like all the good ideas are taken," complained Ben. "We have less than two weeks to put together something interesting."

3   "I know," agreed Akiko. "We just have to keep thinking. Let's sleep on it tonight, and then we'll share any new ideas at recess tomorrow."

4   "Okay," said Ben glumly.

5   The next day, Ben couldn't wait to talk to Akiko. "I have the perfect idea," he told her excitedly. "I was watching the evening news with my parents last night. There was a story about the peregrine falcons in New York City."

6   Akiko looked a little confused. "The falcons actually live in the city?" she asked. "I guess I thought that they would live in places out in the country. Actually, I think I heard that they make their nests on cliffs."

7   Ben nodded. "You're right. But they also live in cities. I guess that tall buildings and bridges seem sort of like mountaintops or cliffs to them. It's more dangerous for them to live in cities, though. That's why people have been helping to protect them. But I haven't even told you the best part yet," he added.

8   Akiko was starting to look excited, too. "What else did you find out?" she asked Ben.

9   "Well, there are about 15 nests in New York City right now. Some of them have 24-hour Web cams set up nearby."

10   Akiko nodded. "I see just where you are going with this idea. We can set up a computer that is hooked up to the Internet. Then, we can show what's happening in the nests right at that moment. This is so original. Mr. Rashad will love it!"

11   Ben looked pleased. "We're going to have the most popular table at the Earth Day celebration."

12   Akiko laughed. "Two weeks seems awfully far away, all of a sudden!"

1. On what day is Earth Day celebrated?

   _____

2. Why do you think it is more dangerous for peregrine falcons to live in cities?

   _____

   _____

3. What is Ben's perfect idea?

   _____

   _____

4. Why does Akiko say that Earth Day seems far away all of a sudden?

   _____

   _____

5. Check the words that describe Ben.

   _____ lonely   _____ boring   _____ excited

   _____ hilarious   _____ enthusiastic   _____ creative

6. On the lines below, write a summary for paragraph 1.

   _____

   _____

   _____

Write the idiom from paragraph 3 on the line next to its meaning.

7. to think about something _____

8. In paragraph 10, Akiko says that their idea is so original. What does she mean?

   _____

   _____

9. Explain what the school's Earth Day celebration activities all have in common.

   _____

   _____

10. Write **C** next to the sentence below that is the cause. Write **E** next to the sentence that is the effect.

    _____ Ben looked pleased.

    _____ Akiko said, "Mr. Rashad will love it."

11. Choose one piece of dialogue from the story, and write it on the line. Tell what the dialogue tells you about the character or the story.

    _____

    _____

Keeping an Eye on Peregrine Falcons

Have you ever seen a peregrine falcon? If you have, was it in a zoo or in the wild?

1   Did you know that the peregrine falcon is one of the fastest animals in the world? It can fly at speeds of about 200 miles per hour. You might think a bird that could fly so fast would be safe from most types of danger. Unfortunately, that is not true. Once, there were about 350 breeding pairs of peregrine falcons in the United States. By the 1970s, they were considered an endangered species. What was causing the number of falcons to drop so quickly?

2   A pesticide, or chemical used to kill insects, called *DDT* was harming the peregrine falcon eggs. It made the shells too thin, and many of the babies could not survive. Luckily, DDT is no longer used as a pesticide. People also began breeding peregrine falcons in captivity. They were finally taken off the list of endangered species in 1999.

3   One thing that is unusual about peregrine falcons is that they like to make their nests in places that are very high in the air. In nature, they often nest on mountaintops and on the sides of cliffs. They have also adapted to life in cities. Peregrine falcons nest on tall buildings and bridges in cities. These nests can be as high as 50 to 200 feet in the air.

4   Pairs of peregrine falcons usually mate for life. They also like to return to the same nesting place every year. Both the mother and father falcons help to raise the babies. The mother spends more time in the nest. The father hunts and brings back food for her and the babies.

5   Many people all around the country work very hard to help peregrine falcons live to adulthood. There are even video cameras set up in places like New York and California to monitor the nests of peregrine falcons. This way, people can make sure that the birds and their eggs stay protected. Many of the cameras even broadcast live in nature centers and on the Internet. The peregrine falcons are lucky to have so many people who care about them.

Write the words from the article that have the meanings below.

1. having babies; reproducing

_____
Par. 1

2. in danger of becoming extinct

_____
Par. 1

3. not in the wild; under someone's control

_____
Par. 2

4. become used to

_____
Par. 3

5. watch closely

_____
Par. 5

6. What caused the falcons' eggshells to become too thin?

_____

7. How high in the air do falcons make their nests?

_____

8. How are the places that peregrine falcons nest in the wild similar to the places they nest in cities?

_____

9. Do you think people will continue to help protect peregrine falcons in the future? Why or why not?

_____

_____

Write **T** before the sentences that are true. Write **F** before the sentences that are false.

10. _____ Only the mother raises the peregrine falcon babies.

11. _____ DDT is harmless to peregrine falcons.

12. _____ Peregrine falcons usually mate for life.

13. _____ Some peregrine falcons are bred in captivity.

14. _____ Peregrine falcons can fly almost 200 miles per hour.

15. What is one way that humans can monitor peregrine falcons?

_____

16. Think about what you know about city wildlife. Name another animal that has adapted to life in the city, and explain how.

_____

_____

Falcons in the City

What kinds of birds do you see in your neighborhood?

1   Salt Lake City, Utah, is famous for many things. It is named for the Great Salt Lake, which is the largest salt water lake in North America. The city hosted the 2002 Winter Olympic Games. Now, it is known for helping to protect a family of peregrine falcons at Temple Square, the headquarters of the Mormon Church.

2   Peregrine falcons usually lay about three or four eggs in a group called a *clutch*. When the babies are about five or six weeks old, they begin learning how to fly. It takes about a week for the parents to teach their fledglings. In natural areas, it is a bit safer for the young birds to take the risks that come with learning to fly. In urban areas, it can be more dangerous because the fledglings can crash into buildings or fly into traffic.

3   In Salt Lake City, volunteers wear bright orange vests to protect themselves as they keep an eye on the young birds. These volunteers actually put themselves in danger to save the birds. For example, if a peregrine falcon fledgling accidentally flies into traffic, one volunteer stops traffic. Another tries to catch the bird and move it out of harm's way.

4   Many birdwatchers in the area heard about the nests and the young falcons. Some of them came out to help. Others just wanted to watch as the babies took their first flights. The volunteers are right to be worried about the young falcons. In the decade of the mid-1980s to the mid-1990s, people counted 16 young peregrine falcons around downtown Salt Lake City. Only 11 of those birds survived. Of the 11 birds, six were helped by volunteers.

5   These numbers help the volunteers remember that the work they are doing really makes a difference. Some of them work 12-hour days to protect the peregrine falcons and their families. However, when the volunteers see a new generation of falcons that are ready to leave home, it makes all their work worthwhile.

Circle the word that best completes each sentence, and write it on the line.

1. It is not as _____ to learn to fly in natural areas.

   fun   dangerous   interesting

2. Young falcons in _____ areas can run into buildings or get hit by cars.

   urban   country   mountain

3. A _____ is a bird that is learning how to fly.

   falcon   fledgling   volunteer

4. Name one thing for which Salt Lake City is famous.

   _____

5. How old are the peregrine falcon babies when they begin learning how to fly?

   _____

6. Why do the volunteers wear bright orange vests?

   _____

7. Why do the volunteers work such long hours to help save the young peregrine falcons?

   _____

   _____

8. Check the phrase that best describes the author's purpose.

   _____ to explain why peregrine falcons don't take good care of their babies

   _____ to entertain the reader with a funny story

   _____ to tell about a group of volunteers who saved some young peregrine falcons

9. A group of falcon eggs is called a _____.

10. In paragraph 4, why does the author say that the volunteers are right to be worried?

    _____

    _____

11. How do you think the author of the article feels about peregrine falcons? Explain.

    _____

    _____

The World of Tomorrow

What are some of the most recent inventions today?

1   "Great Grandpa, what is this?" Henry held a rolled-up poster in one hand. It was yellowed with age and seemed brittle.

2   Great Grandpa was putting price stickers on things that he wanted to sell in his yard sale. "I don't know, Henry. Let's unroll it and find out."

3   Grandpa and Henry slowly unrolled the old poster. They placed it on the folding table in the yard and set a book on each corner to anchor it. The poster revealed a faded picture of a large sphere and something that looked like an enormous spike. Below the picture were the words *New York World's Fair 1939–1940: Building the World of Tomorrow.* Grandpa smiled and gently smoothed the wrinkles in the poster.

4   "Did you go to this fair?" Henry asked Grandpa. "Were you even born yet?"

5   Grandpa laughed. "It does seem like a long time ago," he said. "I was just about your age when I went to the fair. It was one of the most memorable experiences of my life. My parents took me and my sister, Hillary," remembered Grandpa. "It was right after the Great Depression. There was no money for extras for several years. Everything we owned was used over and over again until it fell apart."

6   "What kind of a fair was it?" asked Henry. "The fairs I've gone to have rides and games and fair food, like elephants' ears and caramel apples."

7   "This fair had some of those things, too," nodded Grandpa. "But mostly the 1939 World's Fair was all about technology and things that were new. People in America wanted something to give them hope. They wanted to know that the world was changing for the better and that interesting things were coming their way."

8   "What kind of technology?" asked Henry. "I know that things like computers and cell phones weren't invented yet."

9   "Those types of technology were far off in the future," said Grandpa, "but I did get to see my first television there. It didn't look much like the televisions of today, but I remember how amazed we all were to see a picture moving inside that small box." Grandpa shook his head at the memory.

10   "What are those strange-looking things?" asked Henry, gesturing to the poster.

11   "Those were the biggest attractions at the fair," answered Grandpa. "The Trylon was a 700-foot-tall structure that was shaped like a steeple or a large spike. The Perisphere was a 200-foot-tall building shaped like a ball. Inside the Trylon, people could ride up the world's largest escalator and make their way over to the Perisphere. Inside, I remember seeing a model of an incredible highway system where people could travel at speeds of 100 miles per hour."

12   "Wow!" exclaimed Henry. "That doesn't sound much like the fairs I've been to."

13   Grandpa nodded. "I know. It was a once-in-a-lifetime kind of experience."

1. Number the events below from **1** to **5** to show the order in which they happened.

   _____ Grandpa tells Henry that the fair was about technology and things that were new.

   _____ Grandpa is pricing things to sell at a yard sale.

   _____ Grandpa and Henry unroll the poster.

   _____ Henry says the fair is not like the ones he has visited.

   _____ Grandpa remembers seeing a television for the first time.

2. What major event in history did the 1939–40 World's Fair follow?

   _____

3. Why did Americans want something that could give them hope?

   _____

4. What were the biggest attractions at the fair?

   _____

5. Why do you think Grandpa says the fair was "a once-in-a-lifetime kind of experience"?

   _____

   _____

6. How was the 1939 World's Fair different from the fairs that Henry has been to?

   _____

   _____

7. According to Grandpa, what was life like during the Great Depression?

   _____

   _____

8. Imagine that you are Grandpa, seeing TV for the first time at the fair. Describe your thoughts.

   _____

   _____

   _____

Circle the word that best completes each sentence, and write it on the line.

9. Grandpa _____ the 1939 World's Fair in New York.

   forgot   attended   disliked

10. People wanted to see the _____ technology at the fair.

    latest   oldest   strangest

A Fair to Remember

Have you ever been to a fair or a carnival?

1   Because people are always coming up with important, new inventions, the World's Fairs were started as a way to show all of the latest technology in one place. World's Fairs, also called *International Expositions,* are held every few years in different cities around the world.

2   The first big fair was the Great Exhibition, held in London, England, in 1851. A very large and unique glass building, the Crystal Palace, was built for the event. It still stands in London today. Although most of the pavilions for World's Fairs are not made to last, some still exist. For example, the Eiffel Tower was built to celebrate the centennial of the French Revolution at the Universal Exposition in Paris in 1889. The Biosphere, a giant metal ball, was created for the 1967 exposition in Montreal, Canada. It is still an attraction that people visit today.

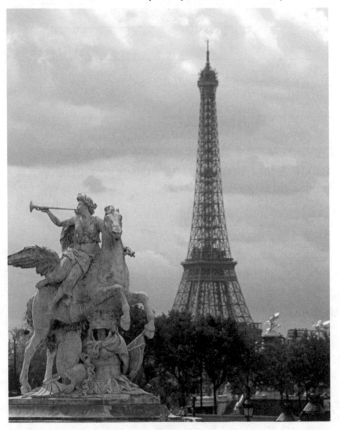

3   Another important building is the Museum of Science and Industry in Chicago. It was built for the 1893 World's Columbian Exposition. It was at this fair that many people saw electricity working for the first time. The fairgrounds were lit up by electric lights. Many of the exhibits showed different uses for electricity.

4   Chicago's fair was also the first World's Fair to have a section of amusement rides. The very first Ferris wheel was there, and it was huge. It stood 250 feet tall, and it could carry as many as 2,160 people! This fair also showed the world that Chicago had recovered from the Great Chicago Fire of 1871. Almost a third of the city had been destroyed at that time.

5   The biggest fair ever held was the 1904 St. Louis World's Fair in Missouri. There were 1,500 buildings. Sixty-two different countries took part. The 1904 Summer Olympics were even held at the fairgrounds! Many people have said that the St. Louis World's Fair is where hot dogs, hamburgers, and ice-cream cones were first eaten.

6   Although there have been many World's Fairs, a few are especially notable. The 1939 New York World's Fair was planned as an event to cheer up people after the Great Depression. It had a time capsule that would not be opened until 6939. It also had one of the very first televisions. The 1939 World's Fair was an important influence on how Disneyland was built.

7   The most popular fair ever held was the 1967 exposition in Montreal. Fifty million people came to see the exhibitions at Expo '67. It was such a hit that the city named its baseball team after the event—the Montreal Expos!

1. Why were World's Fairs first begun?

_____

_____

2. Why was it important for Chicago to host the World's Fair in 1893?

_____

_____

3. Name two structures that were built for a World's Fair but still exist today.

_____   _____

4. How many countries were part of the largest fair in Missouri?

_____

Write **F** before the sentences that are facts. Write **O** before the sentences that are opinions.

5. _____ The Museum of Science and Industry was built in Chicago.

6. _____ About 50 million people came to see Expo '67.

7. _____ The St. Louis World's Fair was the most exciting fair.

8. _____ The 1939 World's Fair had a time capsule.

9. _____ It is more fun to ride the Ferris wheel than any other amusement park ride.

10. Check the line beside the word that tells what type of selection this is.

_____ fiction

_____ fantasy

_____ nonfiction

11. What new technology did many people see for the first time at the World's Columbian Expo in Chicago?

_____

_____

12. What was the author's purpose in writing this selection?

_____ to encourage people to attend World's Fairs

_____ to tell about World's Fairs through history

_____ to describe the first amusement parks

What a Thrill!

Have you ever been to an amusement park? If you have, what was your favorite ride?

1   People have always liked to go on thrill rides. As early as the 1600s, Russians were building giant wooden slides during the winter and covering them in ice. Some were 80 feet tall. People would climb to the top of these slides and then ride down on sleds. Historians think of these rides as the earliest form of what we now call *roller coasters*.

2   The first rides to have cars that ran on tracks appeared in France during the early 1800s. At Frascati Gardens in 1846, the French built the first ride that looped upside down. These were not very fast or long rides, though, and they were not popular for long.

3   In 1872, in the mountains of Pennsylvania, an abandoned railroad track became the first roller coaster ride in the United States. When a coal-mining company built a tunnel through the mountain, a large section of track was no longer needed. It was turned into a thrill ride. The track ran straight down the mountain for 2,322 feet. The speeding train would reach 100 miles per hour. People loved it, and the Mauch Chunk Railway became a huge success. Every year, 35,000 passengers rode the train. It remained very popular until it closed during the Great Depression.

4   LaMarcus Adna Thompson, a very successful inventor and businessman, designed and built the first real roller coaster set in an amusement park. Thompson's "Switchback Railway" opened in 1890 at Coney Island in Brooklyn, New York. Many more coasters were built after people saw how popular this ride could be.

5   In the 1920s, roller coasters were built all over the country. It was a time of great prosperity, called the "Roaring Twenties." People everywhere wanted to have fun and be playful. Then, the 1930s came and brought the Great Depression. Many of the amusement parks were closed because people did not have enough money to visit them. During World War II, lots of the old roller coasters were torn down. The wood and steel were reused in new ways to help fight the war.

6   Today, roller coasters are as popular as ever. You do not have to travel too far to get to an amusement park that has at least one. In fact, if you live in California or Ohio, you are in luck. Six Flags Magic Mountain in Valencia, California has 18 roller coasters and Cedar Point in Sandusky, Ohio has 16!

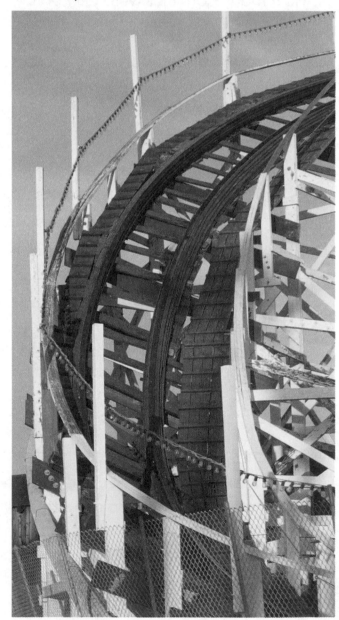

Write the words from the article that have the meanings below.

1. sudden and exciting

_____
Par. 1

2. people who write or study about history.

_____
Par. 1

3. well-liked

_____
Par. 2

4. no longer used

_____
Par. 3

5. success and wealth

_____
Par. 5

6. Which country had the first thrill ride that looped upside down?

_____

7. How many people rode the Mauch Chunk Railway every year?

_____

8. What was the name of the first roller coaster in an amusement park?

_____

9. Why were old roller coasters torn down during World War II?

_____

10. Many amusement parks closed during the Great Depression because

_____.

11. Number the events below from 1 to 5 to show the order in which they happened.
_____ A coal-mining company built a tunnel through a mountain.
_____ The Switchback Railway opened at Coney Island.
_____ The Russians built wooden slides and covered them with ice.
_____ Amusement parks in Ohio and California have the most roller coasters.
_____ Many amusement parks closed during the Great Depression.

12. Check the sentence that best states the main idea of the selection.
_____ Roller coasters are popular again, and you do not have to travel far to find one.
_____ People around the world have loved thrill rides for many years and still do today.
_____ People wanted to have fun and enjoy themselves during the "Roaring Twenties."

The Story of a Quilt

Do any objects in your home tell a story about you or your family?

1   Tess had been in bed with the flu for nearly a week. She was tired of feeling sick and achy. She missed going to school and seeing her friends. She missed playing in the park and going to the library.

2   On Friday, Tess's mom had to go back to work, so Tess's grandmother was coming to stay with her for the day. Tess loved spending time with Nonnie. She was hoping her grandmother would bring some homemade peach ice cream. Nonnie made the best ice cream in the world. Tess waited impatiently for her grandma to arrive. Finally, she heard voices downstairs. A couple of minutes later, Nonnie popped her head into Tess's bedroom.

3   "How's my girl?" she asked Tess. "I heard you were feeling under the weather." Nonnie was carrying a small blue bowl in one hand. A quilt was draped over her other arm.

4   "Hi, Nonnie!" said Tess cheerfully. "Is that peach ice cream for breakfast?" she asked.

5   "How did you know?" said Nonnie. "I thought it might help you get your appetite back." She handed the bowl to her granddaughter.

6   "Why did you bring a quilt with you?" asked Tess.

7   "Well, I thought the quilt might make you feel better, too," said Nonnie. "It was your mother's favorite quilt when she was a little girl."

8   "Did you make it?" Tess asked her grandmother.

9   "No," answered Nonnie, "but my mother and my aunt made it when I was small. This quilt has seen a lot of things," she said softly.

10   Tess rubbed a corner of the quilt against her cheek. "I like this piece best, I think," she said, pointing to a large block of red flowered fabric.

11   "That was from the dress I wore for my sixth birthday," said Nonnie, smiling. "It was my very favorite dress, but I outgrew it by my next birthday."

12   "What about this one?" Tess asked Nonnie.

13   "That piece was from my mother's favorite apron," said Nonnie, gently stroking a small piece of cotton. "She was wearing that apron the day my little brother fell in the creek. She ran out of the house when she heard us screaming for help," remembered Nonnie. "She tore the apron on a rock in the creek, but my brother was okay."

14   "Nonnie, do you have a story for every block in this quilt?" asked Tess.

15   "Almost every one," answered Nonnie. "Now that you know some of them, maybe you will remember and tell your own grandchildren these stories one day."

16   Tess thought for a moment. "Nonnie, you were right. This quilt *did* make me feel better. The peach ice cream didn't hurt, either!"

1. Do you think Tess will ask Nonnie to tell her more stories from the quilt? Why or why not?

   _____

   _____

2. Which piece of the quilt does Tess like best?

   _____

3. What does Nonnie mean when she says, "This quilt has seen a lot of things"?

   _____

   _____

4. How did Nonnie's mother tear her apron?

   _____

   _____

5. What problem does Tess have at the beginning of the story?

   _____

   _____

6. On the line below, write the words that are dialogue in paragraph 12.

   _____

   _____

7. Check the phrase that best describes the author's purpose.

   _____ to entertain the reader with a story about a girl who learns about her grandma's quilt

   _____ to explain how to make a quilt at home

   _____ to tell the reader facts about Nonnie's childhood

Write the idiom from paragraph 3 on the line next to its meaning.

8. not feeling well _____

9. *Tess's grandma is coming to stay with her for the day.* This is the effect. What is the cause?

   _____

10. Tell about something that you or your family owns that has a story behind it.

    _____

    _____

    _____

    _____

Patchwork History

Have you ever sewn anything? Does anyone in your family sew?

1   One of the earliest forms of quilting dates back to the Crusades in Europe in the 1400s. Turkish soldiers wore quilted material under their armor. It kept them warm, but it also added an extra layer of protection. This type of quilted material soon became used for bedding.

2   Quilts are made with two pieces of fabric that have a layer of batting, or padding, stuffed in between them. The layers are then sewn or tied together. Patchwork quilts are made of many tiny pieces of fabric sewn together, often in pretty or interesting patterns. For many years, quilts were made only by hand. Today, many quilts are still handmade, but some are made by machine.

3   Quilting became very popular in America in the mid-1800s. Colonial women did not have a lot of money or resources. Quilting became a way for women to make use of even the smallest scraps of material. They were able to make something practical and beautiful out of material that would have been wasted otherwise. Sometimes, women would trade scraps of fabric with each other to add more variety to their quilts.

4   Quilting bees were popular gatherings. Women did not have many ways to express their creativity, but sewing beautiful quilts was one way they could. They got together in groups from time to time and helped each other with their quilts.

Women worked very hard in the home. They often did not live close to other families, so they spent much time alone in the house. Quilting bees gave them a place to talk and socialize with other women while still completing useful projects. In fact, Susan B. Anthony first talked about women's suffrage, or the right to vote, at quilting bees.

5   The next time you see a quilt, think about all the work that went into it, especially if it was made by hand. Think about each scrap of material coming from a larger piece of cloth that was someone's dress, handkerchief, or shirt. Can you imagine all the stories each quilt has to tell?

1. How did Turkish soldiers use quilted material?

   _____

   _____

2. What is a patchwork quilt?

   _____

   _____

3. What is a quilting bee?

   _____

   _____

4. Why were quilts practical?

   _____

   _____

5. What historical event was Susan B. Anthony a part of?

   _____

   _____

6. How can a quilt tell a story?

   _____

   _____

7. Check the sentence that best states the main idea of the selection.

   _____ A quilt is made of two pieces of fabric with a layer of batting sewn in between.

   _____ Quilting bees were a good place for women to socialize while they were still doing useful work.

   _____ Quilts, which are both beautiful and practical, were a way for women throughout history to reuse scraps of material to make something useful.

8. *All quilts are still made by hand today.* Is this sentence true or false?

   _____

9. The author of this selection is _____ the history of quilts.

   _____ enthusiastic about   _____ bored by   _____ confused by

10. What favorite scraps of fabric would you want to include in a quilt? Explain what they mean to you.

   _____

   _____

   _____

The Mystery of the Quilt Codes

What are some ways to communicate without talking?

1   Quilts can be used to keep warm on a cool night. They can be decorative objects. They can be passed along from one generation to the next. But did you ever think that quilts could be used to communicate, or send messages?

2   Some people believe that quilts made by slaves were used to give information to other slaves who were planning to escape on the Underground Railroad. The Underground Railroad was not actually a railroad. It was the name used for the system that helped slaves travel north, where they could live freely. This trip was very dangerous for slaves. If they were caught, their lives were in danger.

3   Ozella McDaniel said that she had learned the secret codes of the quilts from her relatives. Her ancestors had been slaves. The codes were passed down to her through the generations. The patterns in the quilts contained messages about the journey north. The escaping slaves would memorize the messages so they could take the information with them without being caught.

4   Some of the symbols McDaniel said the slaves used in the quilts were the log cabin, the wagon wheel, the bear's paw, and the star. The log cabin told slaves to look for safe houses. The wagon wheel let them know that they were about to go on a long trip. The bear's paw told the slaves to walk north over the Appalachian Mountains. Also, bears know where to find water and berries. If the slaves ran out of food on their journey, following bear prints could help them survive. The star pattern let the slaves know they should follow the North Star toward freedom.

5   Not everyone believes that slaves used quilts this way. Unfortunately, none of the quilts have survived long enough to prove the stories. Also, the stories were not written down by the slaves. Instead, they were passed down through oral tradition, or storytelling.

6   The historians who study this time in history do not all agree about the meanings of slave quilts. They have different opinions about the purpose of the quilts. We may never know the truth behind the quilts that were made so long ago. However, the work of historians and the legends of storytellers may bring us a bit closer to figuring out the mysteries of the quilts.

Log Cabin   Wagon Wheel   North Star

1. Check the sentence below that is the best summary for paragraph 4.

_____ Some people think that patterns like the log cabin, the wagon wheel, the bear's paw, and the star were used to tell secret codes.

_____ The bear's paw told the slaves to walk north over the mountains.

2. What was the Underground Railroad?

_____

_____

3. What did a star pattern on a quilt mean?

_____

4. Why did the slaves want to travel north?

_____

5. Why don't historians know for certain whether the quilts were used by slaves to communicate information about escaping?

_____

6. Do you think the mystery of the slave quilts will be solved in the future? Why or why not?

_____

_____

7. What is oral tradition?

_____

8. Why do you think oral tradition is less reliable than writing things down?

_____

_____

Circle the word that best completes each sentence, and write it on the line.

9. Quilts may have been used to pass _____ to other slaves.

information   generations   patterns

10. None of the quilts _____ long enough for historians to study.

agreed   survived   proved

11. Some historians have _____ ideas about the purpose of the quilts.

few   studied   different

Make Your Own Quilt

What story do you want your quilt to tell about you?

Things you will need:

- 25 four-inch squares of paper (colored or patterned papers will work best)

- crayons and markers

- glue stick, rubber cement, or two-sided tape

1. First, decide what type of quilt you want to make. You can make two different patterns of squares and alternate them, or you can create your own design. For example, you may want to have alternating squares all around your quilt and a different pattern in the center.

2. Once you have decided what your quilt will look like, you can begin coloring or decorating your squares. Remember that some of your squares can have pictures or symbols on them that are meaningful to you. Your quilt will tell a story about you.

   Here are some ideas of pictures you can include on your quilt squares:

   - your family
   - your pets
   - your friends
   - your house, neighborhood, or school
   - things you like to do
   - places you have visited
   - memories of things that are special to you

   Not every square needs to have a picture on it. You can make a pattern (like polka dots, checks, or swirls) on some pieces, or you can use colored or patterned paper to add variety to your quilt.

3. When you have finished making the quilt squares, spread them out on the top of a large table. Arrange them in an order that you think looks nice. You should have a total of five rows made up of five squares each.

4. Now you can begin attaching the squares to each other, one row at a time. Use a small amount of glue or tape on the edge of each square. When you have five rows completed, you can begin attaching the rows together.

5. If you used glue, allow your quilt time to dry before you hang it up on the wall. See if your friends can determine what story your quilt tells about you.

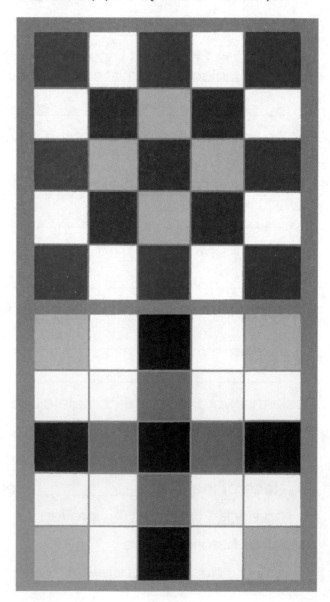

Write the words from the article that have the meanings below.

1. to happen in turns; every other one

_____
Step 1

2. full of importance

_____
Step 2

3. place in a particular order

_____
Step 3

4. figure out; decide

_____
Step 5

5. Check the phrase that best describes the author's purpose.
_____ to persuade the reader that quilts are difficult to make
_____ to explain how to make a paper quilt
_____ to tell about the history of quilts

6. Name two ideas of pictures you could include in your quilt.

_____

7. How big should the squares of paper be?

_____

8. What information should people be able to get by looking at your quilt?

_____

9. Number the steps below from **1** to **5** to show the order in which they appear in the selection.
_____ Decorate your squares of paper.
_____ Decide what type of quilt to make.
_____ Attach the rows of squares using tape or glue.
_____ Arrange the squares on a table.
_____ Gather the materials you will need.

10. Check the line beside the word or words that tell what type of nonfiction selection this is.
_____ biography
_____ how-to text
_____ history

11. What do you need to do before you glue the squares together?

_____

12. A quilt (or paper quilt) can tell a story about you. What other kind of craft or artwork can tell a story about the person who made it?

_____

_____

A Musical Discovery

What kinds of music do you enjoy?

1　*"Ahhhhchoo!"* Devon sneezed. He was helping his great-uncle Frank clean out the attic on a cool fall morning.

2　"It looks like we had better open a window," said Uncle Frank. "I think several years' worth of dust have accumulated up here." The floorboards squeaked as Uncle Frank stepped carefully over a few boxes and opened a small window. He took a deep breath of the crisp fall air and made his way back over to Devon.

3　"Uncle Frank, what are these records from?" asked Devon, holding up a stack of records in white paper sleeves.

4　"Hmm," said Uncle Frank. He picked up the records and looked at the faded dates that were written on the sleeves. "I haven't heard these in ages!" he exclaimed. "I thought they had disappeared years ago."

5　"They look pretty old," commented Devon.

6　"They are very old," agreed Uncle Frank. "Let's go downstairs and see if we can find somewhere to play them. I have a feeling they might surprise you."

7　A few minutes later, Devon and his great-uncle sat on the comfortable old sofa and began listening to the records. The music was strong and clear, and it made Devon want to tap his toes and drum his fingers on the coffee table.

8　"This is great!" he said. "Did you know the people in this band or something?"

9　"Yes, I did," said Uncle Frank with a smile. "I knew them very well. In fact, I married the singer."

10　"Aunt Clara was the singer on these records?" asked Devon with a surprised expression on his face. "I never knew she could sing."

11　"She had a beautiful voice," remembered Uncle Frank. "It was as smooth as honey. I was playing the trumpet in the last song we heard.

Those were some good times."

12　"I never even knew that you and Aunt Clara were in a band," said Devon shaking his head. "Do you still play? What was the name of your band? Were you famous?"

13　"I haven't picked up a trumpet in years," answered Uncle Frank. "Our group was called the *Frank Mack Quartet.* We weren't famous, but in the late 1940s and the early 1950s we were pretty popular at some Missouri jazz clubs. I think I even signed a few autographs when I was young and handsome." Uncle Frank chuckled at the memory.

14　"The best parts of being in that group were meeting your great-aunt and being around people who loved jazz music just as much as we did," said Uncle Frank. "Being famous would have just been icing on the cake."

15　"Uncle Frank," said Devon, "if we find your trumpet in the attic, will you teach me how to play?"

16　Uncle Frank nodded. "Once the jazz bug bites you, there's no going back!"

Write **F** before the sentences that are facts. Write **O** before the sentences that are opinions.

1. _____ Uncle Frank's band was the best jazz band of the century.

2. _____ Devon is helping Uncle Frank clean the attic.

3. _____ Devon should learn how to play the trumpet.

4. _____ Uncle Frank's band played at Missouri jazz clubs.

5. _____ Aunt Clara was in the same band as Uncle Frank.

Write **D** before the phrases that describe Devon and **F** before the phrases that describe Uncle Frank.

6. _____ sneezes because of the dust in the attic

7. _____ has never played the trumpet before

8. _____ thinks Aunt Clara had a beautiful voice

9. _____ has not played the trumpet in many years

10. _____ holds up a stack of records

11. What do you think Uncle Frank means when he says, "Once the jazz bug bites you, there's no going back"?

_____

_____

12. What does Devon want to do when he hears the music on the records?

_____

13. Do you think Devon will learn to play the trumpet in the future? Why or why not?

_____

_____

14. Find the simile in paragraph 11, and write it on the lines below.

_____

_____

15. Write the idiom from paragraph 14 on the line next to its meaning.

something extra; a bonus _____

Trumpet Talk

Have you ever seen someone play the trumpet?

1   Musical horns were given their name for a very good reason: they were made from the hollowed out horns of animals. People found that making a noise at the small end of a tube produced a louder sound at the large end. These horns, as well as some large shells, were the earliest versions of what we now know as the *trumpet*.

2   As far back as the ancient Egyptians, human beings were making trumpets out of silver and bronze. The first horns did not look like the trumpets you might see today. Instead, the tubes were long and straight, not coiled around in a loop. These horns were used for ceremonies, but more importantly, they were used to communicate.

3   The horn was also used for communication in medieval times. Different sections of the army would use the trumpet to tell each other important information, similar to the way more modern armies used the bugle.

4   During the 1800s, the trumpet was finally recognized as an important instrument for musicians. This happened partly because of the introduction of valves to the trumpet. Because the first horns had just a straight tube, the trumpeter could only play certain notes. Coiling the tube into a loop and adding extra tubes to the sides meant that the horn could now make a large variety of sounds.

5   How does a trumpet work? There are three main sections: the mouthpiece, the tubes and valves, and the bell. The mouthpiece is where the trumpeter blows into the horn. This sounds simple, but it is not as easy as blowing up a balloon. The player has to vibrate his or her lips to create the right sound. The mouthpiece is shaped like a cup, so there is room for the lips to *buzz* into the trumpet.

6   This vibration is then carried through the coiled tubes. Pushing down the valves will open the side tubes so that the vibration has to go farther. In a horn, the longer the sound has to go, the lower the note will be. If the trumpeter does not push down any valves, the sound will go straight through the trumpet and produce the highest note. Different valves open tubes of different lengths, so the player can create all of the notes needed for a song.

7   The last part of the trumpet is the bell. This section is where the sound leaves the horn and blasts into the room. The size of the bell also affects the sound. Wider bells produce a softer sound. Narrower bells give off a sharper sound. Some trumpeters even plug the bell with a mute so that the sound is muffled. Miles Davis, one of the greatest trumpeters ever, often used a mute when he played.

Circle the word that best completes each sentence below, and write it on the line.

1. In a horn, the longer the sound has to go, the _____ the note will be.

   higher   louder   lower

2. _____ bells produce a softer sound.

   Wider   Narrower   Older

3. The trumpeter has to _____ his or her lips in the mouthpiece.

   place   vibrate   stop

4. In what way did people in medieval times use the trumpet to communicate?

   _____

   _____

5. Why do some trumpeters use a mute?

   _____

   _____

6. What kind of sound will a trumpet make if the trumpeter does not push down any valves?

   _____

   _____

7. What was one reason the trumpet became recognized as an important musical instrument?

   _____

   _____

8. On the lines below, write a summary for paragraphs 2 and 3.

   _____

   _____

   _____

9. Early horns were made from the _____ of _____.

10. Write one cause from the article and its effect.

   Cause: _____

   Effect: _____

King of the Trumpet

Have you ever played a musical instrument?

1   John Birks Gillespie was born in 1917 in Cheraw, South Carolina. He was the youngest of nine children. John taught himself to play the trombone when he was young and switched to the trumpet when he was 12 years old. After his father died, 18-year-old John and his widowed mother moved to Philadelphia. This was an important move for the young trumpet player. There was a busy musical scene in Philadelphia, and John got a lot of experience performing in public. He also earned the nickname "Dizzy," a name that he would be known by for the rest of his life.

2   Dizzy became well known for the unusual way he played music. He put notes together in a way that no one else ever had. The notes did not seem like they should go together, but somehow the music always worked as a whole.

3   Dizzy also had the opportunity to play with saxophonist Charlie Parker. Charlie was doing new and interesting things on the saxophone the same way Dizzy was doing them on the trumpet. Together, Dizzy and Charlie started a new type of jazz music called *bebop*. Bebop was different than the type of jazz most people were familiar with. It moved more quickly, and the notes were played in an irregular pattern. In the 1940s, the two musicians made several records together. Today, these records are still thought of as some of the greatest in jazz history.

4   There were two things that were especially memorable about watching Dizzy perform. One is that his trumpet looked strange because it was bent. Someone had once accidentally fallen on Dizzy's trumpet. It turned out that he actually liked it better that way and never had it fixed. Dizzy's cheeks also puffed out to look like two small balloons when he played the trumpet. He was a great comedian, so it was always entertaining to watch him perform.

5   Dizzy Gillespie was not just a talented jazz musician. He also cared about social causes. He did some work for the United Nations and eventually even formed a band called the *United Nations Orchestra*. He was also a civil rights activist. He worked to make sure that all Americans would have the same rights, regardless of their race, religion, gender, or social class. Dizzy Gillespie may be best remembered for the ways he changed jazz music. But during his lifetime, Dizzy made a difference in many people's lives.

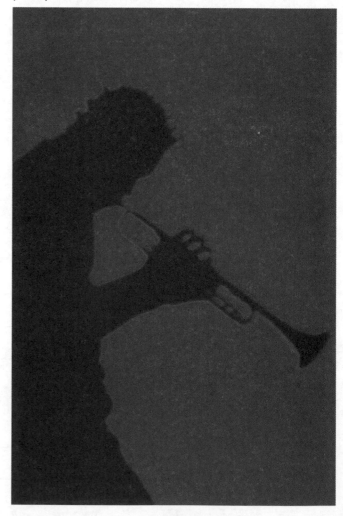

1. How many children were there in Dizzy Gillespie's family?

   _____

2. What instrument did Charlie Parker play?

   _____

3. Name one thing that was different about bebop.

   _____

4. Why was Dizzy's trumpet bent?

   _____

5. How do we know that Dizzy cared about social causes?

   _____

   _____

Read the phrases below. Write **D** next to the phrase if it describes Dizzy, write **C** if it describes Charlie, and write **B** if it describes them both.

6. _____ born in South Carolina

7. _____ played the saxophone

8. _____ made bebop popular

9. _____ played a bent trumpet

10. Check the sentence that best states the main idea of the selection.

    _____ Dizzy Gillespie was a talented musician and a caring person.

    _____ Dizzy Gillespie was the youngest of nine children.

    _____ Dizzy Gillespie played with saxophonist Charlie Parker.

11. Check the words that describe Dizzy Gillespie.

    _____ talented   _____ frustrated   _____ caring

    _____ shy   _____ anxious   _____ musical

12. Do you think people still listen to Dizzy's music today? Why or why not?

    _____

    _____

For the Love of Jazz

Where did jazz music begin?

1   Many people call the United States of America a "great melting pot" where all of the different cultures of its citizens combine to make one diverse culture. A perfect example of this idea is jazz. Jazz began when African American musicians, who listened to a lot of different kinds of music, started to play in a way that combined them all.

2   In the late 1800s, many African Americans who had been slaves were still alive. The songs they had sung while working were based on folk music from Africa. A popular form of this music was hopeful and sad at the same time. It was known as the *blues*. These songs were not written down with notes and lyrics. Instead, the singer or musician would learn the basic melody and then perform it with his or her own personal interpretation. This way of performing is called *improvising*. It is the most important element of jazz music.

3   Originally, jazz was played mostly in New Orleans, Louisiana. Railroads and phonographs helped it become known around the country. Many African American men worked for the Pullman Company, which operated sleeper cars for railroad travel. The men who worked for Pullman told people all around the country about this new, exciting music called *jazz*. They also brought along records, a new invention, so that people could actually hear jazz as well.

4   The trumpeter Louis Armstrong is considered by many historians to be the most important musician of early jazz. In addition to being a fantastic trumpeter, he also made "scat" singing popular. Scatting is when a singer does not sing actual words but uses his or her voice to make nonsense sounds that are more like the music an instrument would make. Ella Fitzgerald was another famous scat singer.

5   During the 1920s, jazz finally became popular with Americans of all races. In fact, it was so popular that the 1920s are still known as the "Jazz Age." Jazz also helped lead to the end of segregation. In the 1930s, the white bandleader Benny Goodman hired an African American pianist and guitarist. At that time, bands were supposed to be all white or all black. Most musicians understood how ridiculous this idea was. No matter how different they might look, deep down they all loved jazz!

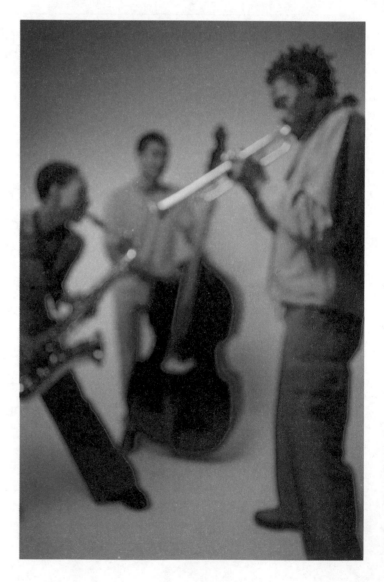

1. Why is America called a "great melting pot"?

_____

_____

2. What are two adjectives the author uses to describe the blues?

_____   _____

3. What two things helped jazz become known around the country?

_____   _____

4. What sorts of sounds does a singer who is scatting make?

_____

5. How did jazz help end segregation?

_____

_____

Write **T** before the sentences that are true. Write **F** before the sentences that are false.

6. _____ The blues are a type of railroad car.

7. _____ The 1940s were known as the Jazz Age.

8. _____ Many African American men worked for the Pullman Company.

9. _____ At first, jazz was mostly played in Georgia.

10. _____ Ella Fitzgerald was a famous scat singer.

11. Explain what improvising is.

_____

_____

12. The author's purpose for writing this article was

_____ to entertain the reader.

_____ to persuade the reader to listen to jazz.

_____ to inform the reader about the history of jazz.

A Bebop Afternoon

Have you ever listened to music at an outdoor festival?

1   Devon, his mom, and his friend Will shook out the checkered picnic blanket. They placed it on the grass under the shade of a large maple tree. Families were setting up all around the park where the jazz festival was taking place. Devon's mom had brought a picnic basket with her, and the boys helped her unload the lunch she had packed. They laid out two kinds of sandwiches, pretzels, apples, lemonade, and fresh brownies.

2   "When do you think the music is going to start, Mom?" asked Devon, helping himself to a turkey and cheese sandwich. He'd been looking forward to the festival for months, ever since Uncle Frank told him that he'd be performing.

3   "It looks like they are almost done setting up," responded Mom. "They'll probably start playing in about 15 minutes."

4   "How long has it been since your uncle played in front of a crowd?" asked Will, biting into a crisp apple.

5   "About 30 years," replied Devon. "We found his trumpet and some old records when we were cleaning out his attic last fall. Uncle Frank started giving me lessons on the trumpet, and he started playing it again himself. He joined the band a couple of months ago."

6   "Is he nervous?" asked Will.

7   "Nope," said Devon. "I think he is just excited. Last week he told me that he hadn't realized how much he missed playing music and being surrounded by people who love it the way he does."

8   "What are they doing now, Mom?" Devon asked. He could hear music coming from the small stage, but it didn't sound like a song.

9   "I think they are just warming up and preparing to begin," said Mom. "You know, your father and I saw Uncle Frank and Aunt Clara perform years and years ago in a club in Missouri. Dad and I weren't married yet. I think it was one of our first dates. That was one of the last times your aunt and uncle performed together."

10   Suddenly, the bandleader tested the microphone. He introduced the members of the band. He even added how happy they were to have Uncle Frank come out of retirement to play again.

11   Devon leaned back and grinned at his mom and Will. The sounds of his uncle's trumpet filled the summer air. He tapped his fingers in time to the rhythm of the music. Devon couldn't wait to learn to play the way his uncle did.

1. Check the phrase that best describes the author's purpose.

    _____ to persuade the reader to learn how to play a musical instrument

    _____ to entertain the reader with a story about a boy watching his uncle perform

    _____ to explain how to play the trumpet

2. Name two things that were in the picnic lunch Mom packed.

    _____ _____

3. Why does Will think Uncle Frank might be nervous?

    _____

    _____

4. Why has Uncle Frank started playing the trumpet again?

    _____

    _____

5. Why do you think Devon grins at his mom and Will at the end of the story?

    _____

    _____

6. Check the words that you think describe Devon.

    _____ curious

    _____ excited

    _____ stingy

    _____ supportive

    _____ angry

    _____ impatient

7. What do the musicians do when they are warming up?

    _____

8. Number the following events from 1 to 4 to show the order in which they occurred.

    _____ Devon and Uncle Frank cleaned out the attic.

    _____ The bandleader tested the microphone.

    _____ Mom saw Uncle Frank and Aunt Clara perform.

    _____ Uncle Frank realized how much he missed playing music.

Plants on the Move

What kinds of plants do you think Beatriz and Abby will discover at the conservatory?

1   On Tuesday afternoon, Mrs. Singh's class walked through the large glass doors of the conservatory. Everyone in the class was supposed to choose one plant that was his or her favorite. When they returned to school, they would write about that plant and share the information they found with the rest of the class.

2   The first room they visited was the rain forest room. The air inside was warm and slightly damp. Beatriz took a deep breath. The air smelled earthy, the way it did in the spring when it had been raining for days.

3   "Is that a palm tree?" Beatriz asked the guide, Mr. Cooney. She pointed to an enormous plant that towered over the room. It had large spiky green leaves that looked a little like the palm trees Beatriz had seen when her family went on vacation in Florida. This tree seemed much larger though.

4   "You're right," said Mr. Cooney. "It is a

type of palm tree. It is called an *Alexandria palm.*"

5   "I like palm trees," Abby told Beatriz, "but I don't think they are my favorite type of plant."

6   In the next room they visited, Mr. Cooney showed the class a *mimosa,* or sensitive plant. "Does anyone know why it is called a sensitive plant?" he asked.

7   Terrell raised his hand. "Because its feelings get hurt easily?" he joked. The class laughed.

8   "Actually, that's not a bad guess," said Mr. Cooney. "Watch what happens when I touch the leaves of the plant." He ran one finger gently down the long spine, and the tiny leaves on either side folded up. "This plant reacts to touch, as you can see, but it also reacts to wind or heat the same way."

9   "Wow," said Beatriz. "I never knew plants could move like that."

10   "What about the Venus flytrap?" asked Abby. "My brother used to have one, and it could move, too."

11   "That's right," said Mr. Cooney. "The Venus flytrap is native to North and South Carolina. The plant gives off a sweet liquid that attracts insects. There are trigger hairs on the inside of the leaves. When an insect touches the trigger hairs, the plant snaps shut and traps the insect inside. Even small animals like frogs can become trapped."

12   "I think the Venus flytrap might be my favorite because it is so unusual," Beatriz said to Abby.

13   "I like the sensitive plant the best," said Abby.

14   "You might not want to make up your minds too soon," said Mrs. Singh, smiling at the girls. "We've only seen a small portion of the plants that are displayed here."

15   Beatriz laughed. "I think I'm going to end up with a whole list of favorites!"

1. What happens if a person touches the leaves of the sensitive plant?

   _____

2. What is another name for the sensitive plant?

   _____

3. Where does the Venus flytrap grow in the wild?

   _____

4. How does the Venus flytrap know that an insect has landed on it?

   _____

5. Do you think Beatriz and Abby will visit the conservatory again? Why or why not?

   _____

   _____

6. Check the sentence below that is the best summary for paragraph 11.

   _____ The Venus flytrap lives in the Carolinas.

   _____ The Venus flytrap attracts and captures insects and small animals.

   _____ The Venus flytrap has sensitive trigger hairs.

Read the sentences below. Write **A** next to the sentence if it describes Abby. Write **B** if it describes Beatriz.

7. _____ Her brother had a Venus flytrap.

8. _____ She didn't know that plants could move.

9. _____ The Venus flytrap is her favorite.

10. _____ The sensitive plant is her favorite.

Write the words from the story that have the meanings below.

11. a greenhouse where plants are grown and displayed

   _____
   Par. 1

12. rose very high in the air

   _____
   Par. 3

13. easily affected by something

   _____
   Par. 6

14. from a particular place

   _____
   Par. 11

Make Your Own Terrarium

What kinds of plants grow well in a terrarium?

Materials you will need:

- a large glass or plastic jar with a lid; a fish bowl covered with plastic wrap will also work

- potting soil

- gravel or small rocks

- small plants that like shade and moisture

1 A terrarium is a great way to have your own miniature garden. It is easy to put one together, and it does not require a lot of care. The lid on the terrarium keeps moisture from escaping. This means that you rarely have to water the plants in your terrarium. After you water the plants the first time, the moisture will evaporate and then condense on the sides of the container. The water keeps getting recycled.

2 Terrariums also do not need a lot of light. When you choose plants for your terrarium, make sure to look for ones that like shade and warm, moist conditions. Here are some examples of plants that do well in terrariums: small ferns, moss, violets, baby tears, and begonias.

A. Place a small layer of gravel at the bottom of the jar or bowl. Then, add a layer of soil to the jar.

B. Now, add the plants to your terrarium. First, decide how you would like to arrange them. Then, make a small hole in the soil and place a plant in it. Pat the soil around the plant to make sure it stays in place. Continue with the next plant.

C. When you have finished planting, you can add a bit of moss or some decorative rocks to your terrarium.

D. Now, place your terrarium in a place where it will receive a bit of sunlight every day. It should not get too much direct light, but it also should not be in complete shade.

E. If you accidentally put too much water in your terrarium, just take off the lid or the plastic wrap for a couple of days. This will allow the extra water to evaporate into the air so that the plants do not rot.

F. If the soil begins to look too dry, you may have to water it a bit. If the plants start getting too large, you can trim them, or you can place them in an even larger terrarium.

G. Now, sit back and enjoy the miniature world you created!

1. Check the phrase that best describes the author's purpose.

   _____ to show that terrariums are the best type of gardens to have

   _____ to tell the history of terrariums

   _____ to explain how to assemble and care for a terrarium

2. What kind of a container can you use to make a terrarium?

   _____

   _____

3. Why don't you have to water the plants in a terrarium very often?

   _____

   _____

4. Name two types of plants that do well in terrariums.

   _____   _____

5. What kind of light will your terrarium need?

   _____

   _____

6. What can happen if you put too much water in a terrarium, and you do not take off the lid to let some of the water evaporate?

   _____

   _____

7. In paragraph 1, the text says, "After you water the plants the first time, the moisture will evaporate and then condense on the sides of the container." What does *evaporate* mean?

   _____

8. What can you do if your plants start getting too large?

   _____

9. Would you like to have a terrarium? Explain why or why not.

   _____

   _____

   _____

A Special Garden

Why do people need to make sure that endangered plants survive?

1   What would you see if you were to go on a tour of the United States Botanic Garden in Washington, D.C.? You would have a chance to see some of the 65,000 plants they care for!

2   Plants are important for many reasons. They provide the oxygen we breathe. They also provide materials for many types of food, shelter, medicine, and fuels that human beings use. One out of every five species of plants in the world is endangered. The people at the U.S. Botanic Garden know how important plants are, so they do their best to raise, conserve, and study plants from all around the world.

3   In 1842, the United States sent an expedition to the South Seas. It was led by Admiral Wilkes. The expedition brought back all sorts of living plants. The U.S. Botanic Garden was founded so there would be a place where the plants could be cared for and studied. The Garden moved to its current location in the Nation's Mall at the foot of the United States Capitol in 1933. In addition to the conservatory, you can visit Bartholdi Park, an outdoor garden that contains about four thousand plants.

4   There are many different areas you can visit at the U.S. Botanic Garden. Each area focuses on a different category of plant. For instance, you might not realize how many plants can grow in the desert. If you visited the Desert House, you could see all kinds of cacti and succulents. These are plants that store water in their leaves so that they can live in very dry places.

5   In the Rare and Endangered House, you would see plants that conservationists worked very hard to find. For example, there is a rare plant called the *Brighamia insignis* that grows on the sea cliffs of a Hawaiian island. Scientists had to climb steep cliffs to gather seeds from these plants to bring back to the U.S. Botanic Garden.

6   In the Medicinal Plant House, you could see plants that are used in making many different medicines. Some of these plants have saved lives. But as more and more of Earth's forests are cut down, there are fewer opportunities for discovering new medicinal plants. There may be plants we have not even discovered yet that hold the key to curing some of the worst illnesses. This is why the Botanic Garden has such an important role in preserving plants.

1. Where is the United States Botanic Garden located?

   _____

2. Name two things plants provide for people.

   _____   _____

3. Who was Admiral Wilkes?

   _____

   _____

4. Why do you think that different categories of plants are located in different areas at the U.S. Botanic Garden?

   _____

   _____

5. How can plants help save people's lives?

   _____

   _____

6. Do you think the U.S. Botanic Garden will continue to grow and preserve new kinds of plants? Why or why not?

   _____

   _____

Write the idiom from paragraph 6 on the line next to its meaning.

7. have the solution_____

Write **F** before the sentences that are facts. Write **O** before the sentences that are opinions.

8. _____ Plants provide the oxygen we breathe.

9. _____ The most interesting plants are the ones in the Desert House.

10. _____ Admiral Wilkes led the expedition to the South Seas.

11. _____ The *Brighamia insignis* grows in Hawaii.

12. _____ The orchid is the most beautiful type of plant at the U.S. Botanic Garden.

13. Describe a garden you've visited. It can be a botanical garden or the garden in your grandparents' backyard. What kind of plants did it have?

   _____

   _____

   _____

   _____

Something in the Air

Why are people so excited to visit the titan arum?

1   When you think about flowers, what sorts of smells do you think of? Most people think of flowers as having a pleasant or even beautiful scent. That is probably because they have never encountered the titan arum, the world's smelliest flower.

2   Not only does it have a strong odor, the titan arum is also the largest flower in the world. In the wild, it can grow to be 20 feet tall with a bloom that is about 6 feet tall and 3 feet wide!

3   Where can you find this unusual specimen? It grows in the rain forests of Sumatra, Indonesia. In the United States, fewer than 20 have been successfully raised in greenhouses and conservatories.

4   It is best known for the awful odor that it produces once the flower has opened. People think the smell is terrible, but insects disagree. In the wild, the smell attracts insects that pollinate the flowers. The bright colors attract birds that eat the seeds. This allows the plant to eventually grow in new places.

5   One reason that this plant is so rare is that both male and female flowers are needed for pollination. Both flowers exist in the large spike in the center of the petals. However, the male and female flowers do not usually bloom at the same time. If another plant is nearby, the flowers can still be pollinated. Because these plants are so rare in the United States, people usually have to help with the pollination process.

6   Another interesting thing about the titan arum is how quickly the bloom dies. People wait years and years to see this amazing plant bloom. Even if a titan arum plant lives to be 40 years old, it may bloom only two or three times. There are usually video cameras that capture every second of the bloom. Television and radio stations have frequent updates. But after only one or two days, the bloom dies.

7   This does not stop people from streaming in for an opportunity to see the plant. During the 18 days before, during, and after the blooming of the titan arum at Huntington Botanical Gardens in California, 76,000 people came to visit this stinky plant!

Today only, smell the **Titan Arum**

1. For what is the titan arum best known?

   _____

2. Where does the titan arum grow in the wild?

   _____

3. Why do you think people are so eager to see the titan arum?

   _____

4. The next time a titan arum blooms in the United States, do you think people will line up to see it? Why or why not?

   _____

   _____

5. Why does the titan arum smell so awful?

   _____

6. Check the sentence that best states the main idea of the selection.

   _____ The bloom of the titan arum lasts only one or two days.

   _____ The titan arum grows in the rain forests of Sumatra, Indonesia.

   _____ The titan arum is fascinating because it is rare, and it is the largest and smelliest flower in the world.

Write **T** before the sentences that are true. Write **F** before the sentences that are false.

7. _____ The titan arum can be found growing in the wild all around the United States.

8. _____ Both male and female flowers exist in the center spike of the titan arum.

9. _____ The titan arum has an awful odor.

10. _____ The bloom of the titan arum can last for two to three weeks.

Write the words from the article that have the meanings below.

11. come in contact with

    _____
    Par. 1

12. a smell

    _____
    Par. 2

13. a sample that is used for scientific study

    _____
    Par. 3

A Family Decision

If you could choose a place for your family to go on vacation, where would you choose to go?

1   "We're having a family meeting," Dad told Juan and Maria. "We have to decide where we'll go on vacation this summer. Start brainstorming places you'd like to visit."

2   A few minutes later, Maria and Juan sat down at the dining room table with their parents. Dad wore a sun visor, sunglasses, flip-flops, and a Hawaiian shirt. Maria and Juan burst into laughter as soon as they saw their father.

3   "Dad, we're not on vacation yet!" exclaimed Juan.

4   "I know, I know," said Dad. "Can you guess where I'd like to go?"

5   Maria nodded. "I'm guessing that you want to go to the beach."

6   Dad grinned. "I thought we could go to Florida. We could swim in the ocean, eat fresh seafood, and collect shells."

7   Mom had a pad of paper in front of her. She wrote down *Dad: Florida (ocean, seafood, shells)*. "Okay, who else has a suggestion?" she asked.

8   "I'd like to go camping," said Juan. "My friend Sophie went camping last year with her aunt, uncle, and cousins. She said they had a great time. They went hiking, cooked-out, and swam in a lake. They had campfires every night and took turns telling scary stories. That's what I'd like to do," said Juan.

9   Mom wrote down *Juan: camping (hiking, cook-outs, swimming, campfires, scary stories)*. "Maria, you're next," said Mom. "Where would you like to go?"

10   Maria thought for a moment. "At the end of the year, my class did a unit about National Parks. Going to Yellowstone National Park in Wyoming would be really interesting. We learned about all kinds of amazing wildlife that you can see there. I'd also love to see the geysers."

11   Mom wrote down *Maria: Yellowstone (Wyoming, wildlife, geysers)*. Then, she put down her pen and looked at the pad of paper. "All of those ideas sound good to me," she said. "I think that camping at Yellowstone might be a good compromise. I know that there isn't an ocean or seafood or shells there," she said, smiling at Dad, "but that way we could do the things that both Juan and Maria want to do on vacation. Also, we went to Florida last year."

12   "You're right," said Dad. "None of us has ever been to Wyoming or seen a geyser. I haven't been camping in years. I think it will be fun to try something new."

13   "Shall we have an official vote?" asked Mom. "Are we agreed that we'll camp at Yellowstone?" Before the words were even out of her mouth, Dad, Juan, and Maria had raised their hands.

14   "Looks like it is unanimous!" laughed Mom. "The Garzas are going to Yellowstone!"

Circle the word that best completes each sentence below, and write it on the line.

1. Dad _____ the family for a meeting.

    gathers   commands   requests

2. Mom _____ everyone's vacation ideas.

    changes   records   ignores

3. Dad thinks that going someplace new would be a(n) _____.

    journey   adventure   mistake

4. Name two things Dad says the family could do in Florida.

    _____   _____

5. Do you think the Garzas will be happy with their decision to camp at Yellowstone? Why or why not?

    _____

    _____

6. How can you tell that Dad wants to go to the beach?

    _____

    _____

7. What problem are the Garzas trying to solve in the story?

    _____

Read each phrase below. Write **M** if it describes Maria. Write **J** if it describes Juan.

8. _____ has a friend named Sophie who went camping

9. _____ guesses that Dad wants to go to the beach

10. In the last paragraph, what do you think *unanimous* means? What detail in the story helped you figure it out?

    _____

    _____

11. What is the setting for this story?

    _____

12. If you could choose a family vacation spot, what would you choose? Why?

    _____

    _____

A Library Expedition

What kind of information do you think the Garzas will find at the library?

1   Juan, Maria, and Mr. and Mrs. Garza were on their way to the library to research what kinds of things they would need for their camping trip to Yellowstone National Park. They were borrowing a tent from Sophie's family, but they weren't sure what other equipment they would need for their trip.

2   When they got to the library, they decided to split up. Juan and Mom were going to look for books about camping. Dad and Maria were going to look for books about Yellowstone.

3   "Let's meet by the reference desk in half an hour," suggested Dad. Then, he and Maria headed over to the travel books, while Mom and Juan sat down at the computers. In just a few minutes, Dad and Maria had pulled out a stack of books about national parks, Wyoming, and Yellowstone.

4   "Can I look through the books about Yellowstone?" asked Maria.

5   "Sounds good to me," replied Dad. "I'll start scanning the ones on national parks and Wyoming."

6   Meanwhile, Mom and Juan made a list of call numbers for books about camping. It didn't take them long to select several books that looked interesting. They spread the books out on a table and began looking through them.

7   A few minutes later, Dad and Maria wandered by with their pile of books.

8   "Wow!" said Mom, looking at all the books on the table. "It certainly looks like we'll have plenty of information to work with here."

9   "Look at this list," said Juan, pointing to a page in the thick green book he was holding. "It's a checklist of the things we'll need for camping. It divides the materials into categories. For example, they have lists of things we'll use for cooking and eating, hiking, and setting up our campsite."

10   "That book seems very practical," said Mom. "I like the way it's organized."

11   "Dad and I found some really great books about Yellowstone Park," said Maria. "This one is by Camilla Jackson. She is a park ranger at Yellowstone. It explains what kinds of clothes we'll need. It can become pretty cold at night. She recommends that we bring lots of layers to wear. There is also a whole chapter in this book about wildlife. I know just what to do if we see a bear. Dad and I can also identify several types of snakes."

12   As the Garzas left the library later that afternoon, Mom said, "We still have a lot of work to do to prepare for our trip, but we got a good start today. We'll just keep on checking things off our lists until we have everything we need. Then, we'll be on the road to Wyoming!"

Write **B** next to the sentence if it happened before the Garzas had chosen their books and met at the table. Write **A** if it happened afterward.

1. _____ The Garzas left the library.

2. _____ Mom and Juan made a list of call numbers.

3. _____ Dad scanned books about Wyoming and national parks.

4. _____ Mom and Juan spread out books on a table.

5. _____ Maria said that they should bring layers of clothes to wear.

Circle the word that best completes each sentence below, and write it on the line.

6. Sophie's family would _____ the Garzas a tent.

   loan   borrow   sell

7. The materials were _____ into categories.

   removed   explained   divided

8. Check the sentence that best states the main idea of the selection.

   _____ The Garzas go to the library to find out how to prepare for their trip to Yellowstone.

   _____ The Garzas agree to meet by the reference desk.

   _____ Juan finds a helpful book that includes different types of checklists.

9. How does park ranger Camilla Jackson suggest campers dress?

   _____

10. Do you think the Garzas will be well prepared for their trip? Explain.

   _____

   _____

11. Have you ever been camping? If so, tell about it. If not, tell why you would or would not like to go.

   _____

   _____

   _____

   _____

The Wolves Are Back!

Why do you think the wolves disappeared from Yellowstone National Park?

1 If you were to take a trip to Yellowstone National Park, there is a good chance that you would be able to catch a glimpse of a wolf during your visit. More than 400 wolves live in Yellowstone National Park today. But if you had visited just a few years ago, you would not have had a chance to see one of these beautiful, independent creatures.

2 Between 1926 and 1995, there were no wolves living in Yellowstone. Because wolves did live there in the past, scientists decided to try to bring them back to the park. In 1995, the United States Fish and Wildlife Service captured 14 wolves in Canada and released them in the park. A year later, they caught and released 17 more wolves. By the third year of the program, 64 wolf pups had been born. The wolves were breeding and raising their young even more quickly than the scientists had hoped!

3 Today, scientists say that Yellowstone National Park has the major predators that it once had before humans interfered. You might wonder why animals that hunt and kill other animals are so important, but everything in nature has a role to play. Think of nature as a see-saw that always wants to be balanced. A big change in nature will cause the "see-saw" to become unbalanced. Human beings, who believed wolves were a dangerous annoyance, caused things to go out of balance at Yellowstone.

4 Scientists call wolves one of the keystone species. This means that many other plants and animals depend on them. Some scientists believe that wolves affect as many as 25 other species at Yellowstone. For example, wolves mostly hunt elk and deer. Other animals that live in the area eat the leftover meat wolves leave behind. This means that those animals may eat fewer plants. More plants grow, and they may be larger than before. This provides shelter for some animals and insects.

5 At Yellowstone, the environment began to change not long after the wolves were brought back. It is quickly becoming more like it was hundreds of years ago. Many people have heard about the program and are interested to hear how the wolves are doing. Scientists are glad that more people are learning about endangered species and how important even a single type of animal can be to the environment.

Write **F** before the sentences that are facts. Write **O** before the sentences that are opinions.

1. _____ Wolves are beautiful creatures.

2. _____ Yellowstone currently has the major predators it had throughout history.

3. _____ Wolves are an annoyance.

4. _____ Wolves mostly hunt elk and deer.

5. _____ More than 400 wolves live in Yellowstone today.

6. What caused the "see-saw" to become unbalanced at Yellowstone?

_____

_____

7. If another species disappears at Yellowstone in the future, what do you think scientists might do?

_____

_____

8. What is a keystone species?

_____

_____

9. Did the environment at Yellowstone begin to change right before or right after the wolves were brought back?

_____

_____

10. What problem did some people have with wolves in Yellowstone?

_____

_____

_____

11. Based on this selection, how do you think the author feels about wolves at Yellowstone?

_____

_____

12. Write one cause from the selection and its effect.

Cause: _____

Effect: _____

Geyser Capital of the World

What do you think creates a geyser?

1   What would you think if you saw water shooting straight up out of the ground? Unless you were near a fountain or a sprinkler, you would probably be quite surprised. When a geyser erupts, however, that is exactly what happens. You would not want to play in its spray, though. The water and steam shooting out of a geyser are more than 212 degrees Fahrenheit!

2   Unless you have taken a trip to Yellowstone National Park, you have probably never seen a geyser. Although single geysers are located in a few places, there are only six spots on Earth where large groups of geysers exist. Geyser fields can be found in New Zealand, Japan, and Iceland, but the largest field by far is in the United States. Yellowstone contains nearly 400 geysers—as many as the rest of the world combined. The geysers at Yellowstone are also among the most active.

3   The word *geyser* comes from an Icelandic word that means *to gush*. Geysers are formed when heated water is trapped deep underground. This water becomes hot when it comes into contact with magma. Magma is a type of rock that is so hot it has turned into liquid. When a volcano erupts, magma comes out in the form of lava.

4   The boiling water and steam in the geyser get trapped because the way to the surface is blocked by cooler water on top. Normally, steam can float away into the air like it does when a pot boils on the stove. The steam in a geyser has nowhere to go. Pressure keeps building until small amounts of cold water are pushed out of the top. Eventually, the pressure from the hot water underground becomes stronger than the weight of cold water on top, and the geyser explodes into the air.

5   Once all of the pressure is released, the eruption ends, and the whole process begins again. Although every geyser is different, the time each geyser takes to erupt can be predicted. For instance, Old Faithful in Yellowstone erupts every 30 to 90 minutes. Each geyser also shoots to a different height. Old Faithful sprays as high as 170 feet in the air. The tallest geyser in the world is Steamboat Geyser, also located at Yellowstone. It can shoot water 350 feet into the air.

6   Today, you do not have to go all the way to Wyoming to see Old Faithful erupt. You can see it from home or school on the Internet. The National Park Service has set up a Web cam that shows Old Faithful in action. Just visit http://www.nps.gov/yell/photosmultimedia/yellowstonelive.htm to see Old Faithful live.

1. Why do geysers erupt?

_____

_____

_____

2. About how often does Old Faithful erupt?

_____

3. Name two places other than Yellowstone where geysers can be found.

_____   _____

4. How far into the air can Steamboat Geyser shoot water?

_____

5. What happens when the pressure of the hot water underground is greater than the cold water on top?

_____

_____

6. Check the sentence below that is the best summary for paragraph 4.

_____ The steam in a geyser has nowhere to go.

_____ Boiling water and steam build up below the cold water until the pressure is too great and the geyser erupts.

_____ When a pot boils on a stove, the steam can evaporate.

Write **T** before the sentences that are true. Write **F** before the sentences that are false.

7. _____ There are almost 400 geysers at Yellowstone.

8. _____ After all the pressure is released, the eruption ends.

9. _____ All geysers shoot water into the air at the same height.

10. Where does the word *geyser* come from, and what does it mean?

_____

11. How do you think Old Faithful got its name? (Hint: Are its eruptions predictable?)

_____

12. How can you see Old Faithful erupting without visiting Yellowstone?

_____

A Natural Beauty

Have you ever visited a national park? Which one would you most like to visit?

1   Who first thought of creating national parks, a place where we could preserve some of the most important parts of our natural and cultural history? Artist George Catlin was one of the first people to have such an idea. He was concerned about the effect of Americans moving westward in the 1830s. He worried about wildlife, wilderness, and Native American cultures in the West being changed as more people moved and the area became more crowded.

2   In 1864, Congress donated Yosemite Valley to California. It would become the first state park. Yellowstone National Park in Wyoming was created in 1872, and many others followed during the next 50 years. The government wanted to preserve these beautiful natural areas. However, the railroad companies were interested in the creation of these parks for different reasons. They wanted more people to travel greater distances. They liked the idea of new tourist attractions all around the country. They also built new hotels near the parks so people would want to visit.

3   Over the years, the types of areas that were preserved expanded. Congress wanted to protect places where there were ancient Native American ruins and artifacts. In 1889, Arizona's Casa Grande Ruin was the first to be preserved. In 1906, Congress passed the Antiquities Act. It allowed presidents to set aside areas that were historically important to our country as national monuments. Theodore Roosevelt created 18 national monuments while he was president. Some of these, like Arizona's Petrified Forest and the Grand Canyon, later became national parks.

4   The national parks were not done growing yet. In the 1930s, the National Park Service was given the monuments of the War Department. This meant that they were in charge of all kinds of historic sites and battlefields. Several years later,

they even added some seashores and lakeshores to the system.

5   Today, there is an enormous variety of things to do and see in the national parks. If you visit Alaska, you can see nearly 50 million acres of national park wilderness. At the Assateague Island National Seashore in Maryland and Virginia, there are bands of wild horses that run freely. In California's Redwood National Park, you can visit some of the tallest and oldest trees in the world. The redwoods there can grow to be more than 300 feet tall and live to be about 2,000 years old.

6   What would have happened to all these places of natural beauty if they had not been preserved as national parks? No one really knows. The important thing is that we remember how lucky we are to have them and do our best to save them for future generations to enjoy.

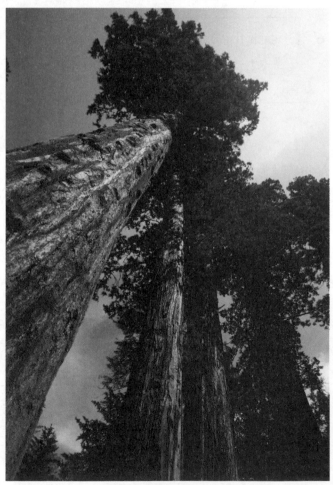

1. Why were the railroad companies happy about the creation of the national parks?

   _____

   _____

2. How tall can redwoods grow to be?

   _____

3. Name one of the national monuments that was created while Theodore Roosevelt was president.

   _____

4. Do you think more national parks will be founded in the future? Why or why not?

   _____

   _____

5. Number the events below from 1 to 4 to show the order in which they happened.

   _____ George Catlin was concerned about people moving westward.

   _____ The National Park Service was given the War Department's monuments.

   _____ Yellowstone National Park was created.

   _____ Congress passed the Antiquities Act.

6. Many historic sites and battlefields are the responsibility of the _____.

7. What is special about the Assateague Island National Seashore?

   _____

   _____

8. Do you agree with the author that it's important to preserve natural spaces? Explain.

   _____

   _____

A **time line** shows the order in which things happened. Use the time line below to answer the questions that follow.

	Casa Grande Ruin		Antiquities Act
Yosemite State Park			National Park Service Bureau created
	Yellowstone National Park		Cape Hatteras National Seashore

1860   1880   1900   1920   1940

9. What year was the Antiquities Act passed? _____

10. Which park was created in 1872? _____

11. Was Yosemite or Yellowstone created first? _____

Mars Mission

Will Max make it to Mars someday?

1   Max had an itch on his knee. It was hard to reach through the bulky astronaut suit he wore. Max unsnapped portions of the suit until he could finally reach the annoying spot.

2   "I sure hope that wasn't a bite from the first flea to travel into space, Winnie," said Max, patting his dog on her head. Winnie wagged her tail and looked up at Max. Max was glad that his dog had been able to come with him on the first manned flight to Mars. He thought about how lonely he would be without Winnie for company.

3   Max checked a number on the brightly lit panel in front of him. "We're almost there, Winnie," said Max excitedly. "If my calculations are correct, we should be arriving on Mars in less than an hour!" Winnie wagged her tail and gave a sharp bark.

4   "You're not getting cold feet, are you girl?" Max asked his dog. "I don't want you to be nervous. We've been preparing for this journey for so long, I know that we'll do fine. Just think, your picture will be in all the history books as the first dog to visit Mars." Winnie just looked at Max. Then, she settled down and rested her chin on her paws.

5   Max turned his attention to the small window. He could see that his ship was rapidly approaching the giant red planet. Max performed one last check of his equipment. "Prepare for landing!" he shouted. Winnie lifted her head for a moment and then rested it on her paws again. There was a loud whooooshing sound, and then an enormous thud as the spacecraft landed on Mars.

6   "We did it, Winnie!" shouted Max, hugging his dog. "We made it to Mars!" Max took his digital camera out of its case and began snapping photos through the porthole. The surface of Mars looked like a rocky, rust-colored desert. In the distance, Max could see something that looked like a massive crater. He tried to position the camera so he could take a photo of it to send back to the scientists at NASA. He was bobbing up and down in the ship when. . .

7   Max opened his eyes. He looked around him. He was bouncing up and down, but he wasn't in a spaceship. He definitely wasn't on Mars. Max was in his own bedroom. Winnie was prancing around on Max's waterbed, which made him feel like he was bobbing up and down. Winnie barked.

8   Max sighed. "It's time for your breakfast, isn't it, girl?" he asked. Winnie barked again. Max started to get out of bed. "It could happen," he said to himself, remembering the rocky red planet and his bulky spacesuit. Max bent down to scratch an itch on his knee. "It could happen."

I. Check the words that describe Max.

_____ competitive

_____ adventurous

_____ curious

_____ imaginative

_____ shy

2. Why was Max glad to have Winnie with him on the spacecraft?

_____

3. What was Max trying to take a picture of when he woke up?

_____

4. In his dream, Max thinks he is bobbing up and down in the air as he is trying to snap a photo. What is happening in real life that makes him think this?

_____

5. On the line below, write the words that are dialogue in paragraph 5.

_____

Write the idiom from paragraph 4 on the line next to its meaning.

6. getting nervous _____

7. How does the picture on page 118 add to your understanding of the story?

_____

_____

8. Describe the setting in Max's dream.

_____

9. What is the setting for the part of the story that takes place in reality?

_____

If the event described takes place in reality, write **R** on the line. If it takes place in Max's fantasy, write **F** on the line.

10. _____ Winnie was trying to let Max know it was time for her breakfast.

11. _____ Max took a picture from the porthole of the spaceship.

12. _____ Max unsnapped parts of his spacesuit.

13. _____ Max got out of bed.

14. _____ Max told Winnie her picture would be in a history book.

The Mysteries of Mars

Do we have neighbors in the solar system?

1   You might not know what a Venusian or a Uranian is, but you have probably heard of a Martian. If there are seven planets besides Earth, why do people commonly think only of Mars when talking about life on other planets?

2   Part of the reason is the Italian astronomer Giovanni Schiaparelli (shee AW pah REL lee). While observing Mars through his telescope in the 1800s, Schiaparelli noticed lines that ran across the surface of the planet. He called these lines *canali*, an Italian word that means *channels*. Schiaparelli used that word because he thought the lines might carry water the way channels, like the English Channel, do on Earth. An amateur American astronomer named Percival Lowell misunderstood what Schiaparelli meant.

3   Lowell read the paper about Mars and saw the word *canali*. He thought that the Italian astronomer meant that he saw canals on the surface of Mars. Canals are human-made structures that carry water from one place to another. Lowell began the theory that an advanced civilization on Mars had built canals all over the planet. He published his articles in newspapers across America. The idea that human beings have neighbors on Mars became very popular.

4   Beginning in 1960, different countries, including the United States, started trying to send spacecraft to Mars. In early 1965, the National Aeronautics and Space Administration, or NASA, launched the *Mariner 4* spacecraft. By July, it was circling Mars and sending back photos and scientific measurements that put a serious dent into any theories about life on Mars. The photos showed a dry planet covered with craters, similar to Earth's moon.

5   *Mariner 9* was launched in 1971. It showed a different part of the planet. This area of Mars had volcanoes, canyons, and mysterious channels that once might have carried water. Scientists knew that if the planet had once had flowing water, there was at least a chance that it also might have had life. The scientists now needed to prove that Mars once had water.

6   In January of 2004, NASA landed two spacecrafts on Mars, *Spirit* and *Opportunity*. Called *rovers*, they were equipped with very advanced tools. They could drive around on the planet but be controlled by scientists on Earth. They made an amazing discovery. The rocks that the rovers picked up and examined showed the scientists that Mars did have flowing water in the past. The news excited scientists worldwide. Another rover, named *Curiosity*, landed on Mars in 2012. Today, it continues the search for life on Mars.

1. What did Percival Lowell think Schiaparelli saw on the surface of Mars?

   _____

2. What was the name of the American spacecraft that was sent to Mars in 1965?

   _____

3. Do you think that scientists will continue to look for life on Mars? Why or why not?

   _____

   _____

4. In the passage, what problem did Percival Lowell have?

   _____

   _____

5. Does this selection take place in reality, or is it a fantasy? How can you tell?

   _____

   _____

6. Check the phrase that best describes the author's purpose.

   _____ to explain why there is no life on Mars

   _____ to tell about the search for life on Mars

   _____ to persuade the reader to visit Mars someday

Read each sentence below. If the event took place before 1965, write **B** on the line. If it took place after 1965, write **A** on the line.

7. _____ *Spirit, Opportunity*, and *Curiosity* landed on Mars.

8. _____ Schiaparelli noticed lines that ran across the surface of the planet.

9. _____ Lowell created the theory about canals and civilization on Mars.

Write the words from the article that have the meanings below.

10. an expert in the study of the universe

   _____
   Par. 2

11. watching closely

   _____
   Par. 2

12. ahead of its time

   _____
   Par. 3

Space Travelers

Do you have what it takes to be an astronaut?

1   Although it is still rare, space travel is becoming more and more common. There have now been 536 people from more than 38 countries who have flown in space. In English-speaking countries, they are known as *astronauts*. This word comes from the Latin words *astrum*, which means *star*, and *nauta*, which means *mariner*, or the person who plots the course of a ship. You have to fly more than 62 miles above Earth to officially be in space!

2   The first human to fly in space was a *cosmonaut*, the Russian word for *astronaut*. In April 1961, cosmonaut Yuri Gagarin orbited Earth in the spacecraft *Vostok 1*. Only one month later, Alan Shepard became the first American astronaut, although he did not fly completely around the planet. John Glenn was the first American to do that. He orbited Earth three times in 1962. He also became the oldest astronaut when he returned to space in 1998 at the age of 77. The first woman to fly in space was also a Russian cosmonaut. Valentina Tereshkova went into space on *Vostok 6* in June of 1963.

3   At first, almost all astronauts were pilots. The earliest space flights were made just to see if humans could make the journey into space. For this reason, the main job for the astronaut was flying the spacecraft. Today, astronauts need to be able to perform many more tasks. They do not just fly space shuttles. They also take part in planning the flights and the experiments. Astronauts are now scientists, engineers, medical doctors, and sometimes pilots as well.

4   To be an astronaut, the first thing you need is a college education. Your degree should be in math, science, or engineering so that you are able to plan experiments or operate the computer controls on the shuttle. You should also be in great physical condition because space flight is hard on the human body. If you want to be a shuttle pilot, you also need incredible

eyesight and at least one thousand hours of flying experience. All astronauts need to be trustworthy, reliable, and excellent communicators.

5   If you have met all of those requirements, you are ready to start astronaut training. For at least a year, astronaut candidates learn how the shuttle works, how to survive crashes, and how it feels to be in outer space. They train inside a simulator, which is like a very realistic computer game that looks and feels like the inside of the shuttle. Pilots also practice landing the shuttle by flying an STA, or Shuttle Training Aircraft.

6   Even after astronauts have finished their training, they still do not fly right away. New astronauts will first take part in planning experiments, testing computer software, and helping to prepare the launch site. Eventually, the day arrives when they are selected to go on a flight!

1. What is the first thing you need to do if you want to become an astronaut?

   _____

2. What was the profession of most of the first astronauts?

   _____

3. Why do you need to be in good shape to be an astronaut?

   _____

4. Why do you think astronauts need to be good communicators?

   _____

5. What is a simulator?

   _____

6. On the lines below, write a summary for paragraph 4.

   _____

   _____

   _____

7. Write **T** before the sentences that are true. Write **F** before the sentences that are false.

   _____ New astronauts can fly as soon as they have finished their training.

   _____ Today, astronauts need to be able to perform many tasks.

   _____ Alan Shepard was the oldest astronaut to go into space.

   _____ If you fly 40 miles above Earth, you are officially in space.

   _____ You need to have good eyesight to be a shuttle pilot.

8. Name characteristics that an astronaut needs to have.

   _____

   _____

9. _____ was the first American to orbit Earth.

10. Do you think you would make a good astronaut? Why or why not?

   _____

   _____

A Friendly Lesson

Have you ever been afraid of something but tried to do it anyway?

1   Maggie sat dangling her feet into the sparkly blue water of her family's swimming pool. She had been anticipating the new pool for months. Now that it was there, though, she didn't feel as happy as she thought she would.

2   "What's wrong?" asked her mom.

3   Maggie sighed. "Amelia is scared of the water. She doesn't know how to swim. I thought that she would be playing with me in the pool all summer. I miss Amelia. Nothing is as much fun without her," said Maggie, lightly splashing water over her knees.

4   "Hmmm," said Mom. "Why don't you go call Amelia and see if she can come over? Maybe if you and I both get in the pool with her, we can help her feel safe in the water. Remember how we taught your little brother to swim? Now, he swims like a dolphin!"

5   Maggie looked a little more cheerful. "You're right, we did teach Tyler to swim. He was pretty scared the first time we took him to the pool, wasn't he?" asked Maggie. "I think I'll go call Amelia right now and see if her dad can bring her over."

6   Later that afternoon, Amelia came over with her dad. "Are you sure you don't want me to stay?" he asked.

7   Amelia nodded. "I think I'm ready to do this," she said. "I'm tired of being scared of the water. I don't want to miss a whole summer of swimming with Maggie."

8   "I'm proud of you," said her dad. "I'll be back in a couple of hours, okay?" Amelia nodded again and sat on the side at the shallow end of the pool.

9   All afternoon, Maggie and her mom worked with Amelia in the water. They taught her how to blow bubbles so she wouldn't get water in her nose. They taught her to kick across the width of the pool holding a kickboard. When Amelia's dad came to pick her up, everyone was surprised the time had gone so quickly.

10   "Watch this, Dad!" shouted Amelia. "I can float on my back. Maggie's mom can even let go for a few seconds, and I can do it on my own!" She proudly demonstrated her new skills for her father.

11   "This is amazing!" said Amelia's dad. "You two must be incredible teachers."

12   Maggie and her mom smiled at each other. "I think Amelia was just ready to learn," said Maggie's mom. "She set her mind to it and did all the work herself."

13   "Can we come back tomorrow, Dad?" asked Amelia. Everyone laughed.

14   "I have a feeling that I'm going to have a prune for a daughter all summer!" said Amelia's dad.

1. Check the words that describe Amelia.

   _____ funny

   _____ brave

   _____ determined

   _____ suspicious

   _____ proud

Circle the word that best completes each sentence, and write it on the line.

2. Mom and Maggie helped Amelia _____ her fear of the water.

   ignore   overcome   explain

3. Maggie _____ Amelia's company.

   enjoys   dislikes   forgets

4. Amelia's dad had not _____ her to learn so much in one afternoon.

   wanted   expected   selected

5. Why does Maggie feel sad at the beginning of the story?

   _____

6. What does Dad mean when he says, "I'm going to have a prune for a daughter all summer"?

   _____

7. Why does Amelia want to learn how to swim?

   _____

   _____

8. Why does Amelia say that she wants to come back tomorrow?

   _____

   _____

Find the simile in paragraph 4, and write it on the line below.

9. _____

10. Why did it make a difference that Amelia was finally ready to learn?

   _____

   _____

11. Tell about something that you tried, even though it made you uncomfortable at first.

   _____

   _____

   _____

Sink or Swim

Why do things float?

Materials:

- a large bowl of water
- an apple
- a carrot

1   What do you think will happen when you place the apple and the carrot in the water? Will they sink or float?

2   Put the carrot and the apple in the bowl one at a time. The carrot will sink, but the apple will float. This is because apples and carrots contain different amounts of air. Air is lighter, or less dense than water. Something that contains more air will float better than something that is denser.

3   The cells of a carrot are packed together tightly. There is more air in the cells of the apple. This allows the apple to float and causes the carrot to sink.

Materials:

- two clear glasses
- warm water
- two grapes
- 3 teaspoons salt
- a spoon

4   Now, think about salt water. Do you think that things are more or less buoyant in salt water than in fresh water?

5   Fill both glasses with warm water. Then, add the salt to one glass. Stir the water until the salt dissolves. Now, place one grape in each glass of water. The grape in the glass of fresh water will sink. The grape in the glass of salt water will float. How is this possible?

6   The weight of the grapes is not different. If something is heavier than the same volume of water, it will sink. If something is lighter, it will float. Salt water is heavier, or denser, than fresh water. This means that it can support heavier things than fresh water can.

7   If you ever visit the Dead Sea near Israel, you can try this experiment with your own body. The human body is made mostly of water. The Dead Sea is much saltier than other oceans. In fact, it contains more than 30 percent salt and minerals. In comparison, the Pacific Ocean only has about 3 percent salt and minerals. Because the Dead Sea is so salty, your body is much less dense than the water. This means you could float without even trying!

Circle the word that best completes each sentence, and write it on the line.

1. Salt water is _____ than fresh water.

   denser   colder   deeper

2. Something that is _____ than the same volume of water will sink.

   older   heavier   stronger

3. The Dead Sea is _____ than the oceans of the world.

   lighter   fresher   saltier

4. Check the phrase that best describes the author's purpose.

   _____ to explain how to conduct two experiments about floating

   _____ to persuade the reader to become a scientist

   _____ to show why the water in the Dead Sea is so salty

5. Why do you think you need to use warm water in the second experiment?

   _____

   _____

6. Why does the apple float while the carrot sinks?

   _____

   _____

7. What do you think would happen if you used an egg instead of a grape in the second experiment?

   _____

8. Where is the Dead Sea located?

   _____

Write the words from the article that have the meanings below.

9. packed tightly together; heavy

   _____
   Par. 2

10. able to float

   _____
   Par. 4

11. melts; turns from a solid into a liquid

   _____
   Par. 5

Flood Watch!

How will the Lopez family keep their basement from flooding?

1   Teresa and Manuel sat on the couch in the living room. They could not think of a single thing to do. It had been raining steadily for four days. Teresa and Manuel had done all the rainy day activities they could think of.

2   They played games. They set up easels and painted. They made cookies. They watched all their favorite movies. They even helped their mom clean out all the closets in the house. They were out of ideas.

3   Mr. Lopez walked by carrying a basket of laundry. He stared at Manuel and Teresa slouched on the couch. "What are you kids doing?" he asked.

4   "There is absolutely nothing left to do in this house!" said Teresa dramatically. "It may never stop raining!"

5   "All we want to do is go outside," agreed Manuel. "It feels like we haven't left the house in a month."

6   "I'm sure I can think of something…"

began Mr. Lopez. Just then, Mrs. Lopez came running into the room.

7   "I was just listening to the local news on the radio," she said. "Sawmill Creek is rising very quickly. It's already overflowed its banks in some places. The rain isn't supposed to let up anytime soon, so it's probably going to flood in our neighborhood, too. I think it's time for us to sandbag the house." Teresa and Manuel sat up. They were excited to have something finally happen!

8   "Kids, if you want to help, you need to put on your rain jackets and boots," said their dad. "If we hurry, we may be able to keep the basement from flooding too badly."

9   The Lopez family quickly put on their rain gear and headed outside. The small creek that normally trickled quietly behind their house was rushing loudly now. The grass squished under their feet as they walked across the lawn toward the garage. Mr. Lopez grabbed several large bags that were on a shelf in the garage.

10   "Okay, Teresa and Manuel, you can start filling the bags with sand from these containers," said Mr. Lopez. Mom and I will carry the bags outside and start piling them around the base of the house."

11   "Won't the water leak around the bags?" asked Teresa.

12   "Maybe a little," said Mom. "But we're going to overlap the bags so that there aren't any gaps between them. Then, we're going to cover the bags with sheets of plastic. That will help make them even more watertight."

13   After a few trips, Dad paused and grinned at Manuel and Teresa. "You said you wanted to get out of the house. This isn't what you had in mind, is it?"

14   Manuel and Teresa laughed. "No, but at least it's more exciting!" said Manuel.

1. Name two rainy day activities Teresa and Manuel did.

_____

_____

2. Why did the grass squish beneath their feet as they walked across it?

_____

3. Where did Mrs. Lopez hear the news that Sawmill Creek was flooding?

_____

4. If the story continued, what do you think would happen next?

_____

_____

_____

5. Name one way that Teresa and Manuel are similar.

_____

_____

_____

Write **F** before the sentences that are facts. Write **O** before the sentences that are opinions.

6. _____ At the beginning of the story, Teresa and Manuel are bored.

7. _____ Keeping the basement from flooding is exciting.

8. _____ Sawmill Creek is rising quickly.

9. _____ Mom and Dad overlap the sandbags so there are not gaps between them.

10. _____ Rainy days are boring.

11. Why does the family need to sandbag the house?

_____

_____

12. Mom hopes that covering the bags with plastic will make them more

_____.

The Flood of the Century

What contributed to the disaster of the Johnstown Flood?

1 The city of Johnstown is located in southwestern Pennsylvania. In the late 1800s, it was a nice, quiet place to live, with a steel company that employed many of its citizens. The town was built on a floodplain, but most people did not pay too much attention to that fact. As the town grew, it moved closer and closer to the banks of Stony Creek and the Little Conemaugh River.

2 South Fork Dam lay 14 miles upstream from the city of Johnstown. It held Lake Conemaugh on the side of a mountain, 450 feet above the city of Johnstown. The South Fork Fishing and Hunting Club owned the dam. They had turned the lake into a resort area. The dam was not in good repair, but the club did not have it fixed. Some people worried that one day, the dam would no longer be able to hold back the water, but nothing was done in time to save the town.

3 On May 31, 1889, after heavy rains, the dam burst. It sent 20 million tons of water rushing down the Little Conemaugh River at speeds of about 40 miles per hour. As it approached Johnstown, the wall of water was nearly 60 feet tall in some places.

4 The people of the town were caught by surprise. Many tried to escape, but the water moved too quickly. Some people managed to climb onto pieces of debris and use them as rafts. Some were able to survive by hiding in their attics until help could reach them. Others were not so lucky. The Johnstown Flood ended up taking the lives of 2,209 people.

5 It took years for the city of Johnstown to clean up the mess created by the disaster. It took even longer for the people to recover from the loss of so many lives. Some people blamed South Fork Fishing and Hunting Club for not keeping the dam in good repair. They believed that if the dam had been maintained, it might have saved the lives of many people who drowned during the Johnstown Flood.

6 Today, you can visit the Johnstown Flood National Memorial in southwestern Pennsylvania. There is a 165-acre national park there, as well as the remains of the South Fork Dam. You can see photos of Johnstown before and after the flood. It is sad to see the wreckage the flood created. Even so, the fact that Johnstown exists today shows the strength and determination of people who faced one of the worst disasters in American history.

1. Who owned South Fork Dam at the time of the flood?

_____

2. Why does the author say that the fact that Johnstown exists today shows the strength of people in that town?

_____

_____

3. What problem did the people of Johnstown have in the selection?

_____

_____

4. Number the events below from **1** to **5** in the order in which they happened.

_____ Some people were worried that the dam might not hold.

_____ The dam sent 20 million tons of water rushing down the Little Conemaugh River.

_____ The Johnstown Flood National Memorial was founded.

_____ The South Fork Fishing and Hunting Club bought the South Fork Dam.

_____ The people of the town were caught by surprise.

5. Check the sentence that best states the main idea of the selection.

_____ The water flooded Johnstown at speeds of about 40 miles per hour.

_____ The city of Johnstown is located in southwestern Pennsylvania.

_____ The Johnstown Flood in 1889 was one of the worst disasters in American history.

6. Check the line beside the word or words that tell what type of nonfiction selection this is.

_____ biography

_____ history

_____ how-to text

7. Does this story take place in reality, or is it a fantasy? How can you tell?

_____

_____

8. What do you think the purpose of the Johnstown National Memorial is?

_____

9. The picture on page 130 looks like a black and white photo from a newspaper. How does the artwork help you understand the story better?

_____

_____

Career Day

Have you ever thought about what kind of career you might like to have as an adult?

1 Hiroshi sat at the kitchen table. He stared at the blank sheet of paper in front of him. Then, he stared out the window. For a homework assignment, Hiroshi was trying to decide what kind of career he wanted to have. Once he chose a career, he was supposed to research it so he could share the information with the rest of the class.

2 Hiroshi wasn't sure what he wanted to be. When he was younger, he thought that he might like to be a firefighter. Hiroshi liked the idea of helping people. He also liked the trucks firefighters drove and thought that it would be an exciting job. After Hiroshi went to his first professional baseball game the summer before, he thought he might like to play baseball professionally. He knew that becoming a professional ballplayer was a long shot, so he wanted to think of some other ideas that were more realistic.

3 When Hiroshi's sister Saki came into the kitchen for a snack a few minutes later, Hiroshi was still sitting there with the blank piece of paper in front of him.

4 "What are you doing?" she asked, grabbing a green apple and a handful of cheese crackers.

5 "I need help," said Hiroshi. "I'm trying to think of things that I might like to do for a career. I don't know where to start."

6 Saki shrugged. "That doesn't sound too hard," she said, taking a bite of her apple. "I thought your class went on a field trip to a Frank Lloyd Wright building a few months ago and you decided you wanted to be an architect."

7 "I forgot all about that trip!" exclaimed Hiroshi. "I thought that Fallingwater was amazing. I've never seen another building like that. It felt like the house was part of the forest and the waterfall was part of the house."

He grinned at his sister. "I would love to design buildings like that." Hiroshi wrote down *architect* at the top of his paper.

8 "And didn't you tell Mom and Dad that you wanted to be an oceanographer after you saw that biography of Jacques Cousteau on TV?" asked Saki.

9 Hiroshi nodded. "I can't believe you remembered that," he said. "That would be an amazing job, too. There are so many things that humans don't know about the ocean yet. I like the mystery of it." He added *oceanographer* to his list.

10 "I also seem to remember that someone wanted to be a clown when he was little," teased Saki.

11 Hiroshi laughed. "Sometimes, I wish you didn't have such a good memory. Thanks, but I think I'll stick with the first two careers on my list."

1. What is Hiroshi's homework assignment?

   _____

   _____

2. What did Hiroshi like about Fallingwater?

   _____

   _____

3. How does Saki tease her brother at the end of the story?

   _____

4. What made Hiroshi want to be an oceanographer?

   _____

5. On the line below, write the words that are dialogue in paragraph 4.

   _____

Read the sentences below. Write **H** next to the sentence if it describes Hiroshi. Write **S** if it describes Saki.

6. _____ eats a green apple

7. _____ wanted to be a firefighter

8. _____ has a good memory

9. _____ likes the mystery of the ocean

10. _____ makes a list of career ideas

Write the idiom from paragraph 2 on the line next to its meaning.

11. something that is not likely _____

12. Do you think it's wise of Hiroshi to choose a more practical career than being a professional baseball player? Explain.

    _____

    _____

    _____

13. If you had to write about a career and research it, what would you choose? Why?

    _____

    _____

    _____

The Wright Stuff

What is the most unusual building you've ever seen?

1   Many people think that Frank Lloyd Wright was the most important architect of the twentieth century. He introduced new ways of thinking about architecture. Wright believed that buildings should not just be big boxes with doors and windows. He thought that a building's shape should fit in with its natural environment.

2   Wright also wanted to make sure that people would always be able to experience the natural world, even when inside a building. For these reasons, Wright's building style was called "organic architecture."

3   Frank Lloyd Wright was born in 1867 and grew up in Wisconsin. In 1887, when he was twenty, he moved to Chicago, Illinois, to work and learn at an architecture firm. After only five years, Wright was ready to go out on his own as a designer. Many of his buildings can be found in Illinois, although he built all over the world.

4   One of his early and very popular designs was called the prairie house. This style of house is a great example of organic architecture. Wright wanted to design a house that imitated the landscape of Illinois and the rest of the Midwest. The middle section of the United States is mostly flat farmland that was originally prairie. For this reason, the prairie houses were very flat and spread out. People loved the way they looked!

5   Wright's most famous house might be Fallingwater in Pennsylvania. This house was built right on top of a stream and waterfall! A stairway leads from the living room right down to the water. Wright also wanted to make sure that the surrounding woods would be a major part of the house. By putting lots of windows in every room, the outdoors would always be visible.

6   Homes were not the only things Wright designed. The headquarters for the Johnson Wax Company is another famous building. This time, Wright used a forest as inspiration for the main work area inside. The large room has many towering columns that become thinner as they reach the ceiling, imitating the way tree trunks grow smaller toward their tops.

7   The last building Wright completed during his lifetime was the Guggenheim Museum in New York City. Many people think it is his masterpiece. Wright's design for the museum is based on the spiral shape of a shell. Both the inside and the outside of the building loop around like a spring. Wright's interesting and unusual museum is far from looking like a box, which is just the way he wanted it.

Frank Lloyd Wright found inspiration for his buildings in the natural world.

1. How were the prairie houses similar to the landscape of the Midwest?

    _____

    _____

2. How do you think Fallingwater got its name?

    _____

    _____

3. What is the shape of the Guggenheim Museum in New York City?

    _____

4. What do you think Wright's feelings about the natural world were?

    _____

5. Check the sentence below that is the best summary for paragraph 4.

    _____ One of Wright's most popular designs was the prairie house, which imitated the Midwest landscape.

    _____ The Midwest contains many areas of flat farmland.

6. Check the words that describe Wright.

    _____ imaginative   _____ unique

    _____ talkative   _____ rude

    _____ creative

7. Check the line beside the word or words that tell what type of selection this is.

    _____ biography   _____ myth
    _____ how-to

8. Write the sentence that is a caption on page 134.

    _____

    _____

9. *Wright believed that buildings should basically look like boxes with windows.* Is this true or false?

    _____

10. A _____ was the inspiration for Wright's Johnson Wax Company headquarters.

The World Underwater

How do you think the wreckage of the Titanic *was discovered?*

1   People are fascinated by the exploration of space. They like the idea that so many things about our solar system are a mystery. But there are still some very mysterious places on Earth that have not been explored yet. The ocean is one of those places, and Robert Ballard is one of its lucky explorers.

2   Robert Ballard was born in 1942 in Kansas. He grew up in San Diego, California, where he first developed an interest in the ocean and ocean life. One of his favorite books as a child was Jules Verne's *20,000 Leagues Under the Sea*. That novel, and the influence of his parents, are two of the most important reasons Ballard wanted to become an undersea explorer.

3   As a young man, Ballard earned degrees in chemistry and biology. He also spent some time in the Navy, working as a marine biologist. After he left the Navy, Ballard returned to school, where he studied geology and geophysics. Then, Ballard spent several years mapping underwater mountain ranges on the ocean floor.

4   One of the most interesting discoveries Ballard made was of giant worms on the ocean floor. The tubeworms, called *Riftia*, were an important discovery because scientists did not think that any organisms could survive so deep underwater. Nearly all forms of life need the energy of the sun. The sun's rays do not reach all the way to the dark ocean floor, so scientists thought that no plants or animals could live there.

5   While on a trip to the Galápagos Islands in 1977, Ballard discovered worms that were more than 10 feet long. They lived near underwater hot springs and received energy from the springs rather than from the sun. This discovery changed scientists' ideas about life on this planet, as well as on other planets.

6   In 1985, Ballard finished work on his first remote-controlled robot, *Argo*. *Argo* changed the way the underwater world was explored. Now, remote-controlled underwater cameras could take photographs and send the pictures to computers on the surface. *Argo* helped Ballard with the discovery of the luxury ocean liner the *Titanic* in 1985, his most well-known accomplishment.

7   The *Titanic* struck an iceberg on her maiden voyage in 1912. More than 1,500 people lost their lives when the enormous ship sank. Ballard was part of the crew that used sonar to discover the wreckage of the *Titanic* more than 12,000 feet underwater. Ballard then had to wait an entire year before weather conditions were good enough for exploring one of the most famous shipwrecks of all time.

8   Robert Ballard's childhood dreams of being an undersea explorer came true. His talent, hard work, and imagination have allowed him to see some amazing parts of the Earth that few people ever experience.

Write **F** before the sentences that are facts. Write **O** before the sentences that are opinions.

1. _____ Robert Ballard is the greatest living scientist today.

2. _____ Ballard grew up in San Diego.

3. _____ More money should be spent on space exploration than on ocean exploration.

4. _____ The *Titanic* sank on her maiden voyage in 1912.

5. _____ Ballard discovered tubeworms near the Galápagos Islands.

6. What is one way in which outer space and the oceans are similar?

_____

7. Why was Ballard's discovery of deepwater tubeworms so important?

_____

_____

8. What did *Argo* send back to the surface from deep underwater?

_____

9. Why did Ballard have to wait a year before exploring the *Titanic*?

_____

10. Who is the author of the novel *20,000 Leagues Under the Sea*?

_____

Write the words from the article that have the meanings below.

11. very interested in

_____
Par. 1

12. making a map of

_____
Par. 3

13. something expensive and pleasurable that isn't really necessary

_____
Par. 6

14. a device that uses sound waves to find underwater objects

_____
Par. 7

E-mail Advice

What is it like to be an architect?

From: Hiroshi Ishikawa
Date: November 13, 2014
To: Mr. Daley
Subject: Architect career

Dear Mr. Daley,

¹   My aunt said that you would be expecting to hear from me. My name is Hiroshi, and I am interested in becoming an architect. I would like to learn more about what it is like to be an architect. Can you tell me a little more about your career? What do you like best about it? I would be happy to receive any advice you have.

²   Thank you for your time. I look forward to hearing from you.

Sincerely,

Hiroshi Ishikawa

From: Andrew Daley
Date: November 15, 2014
To: Hiroshi Ishikawa
Subject: RE: Architect career

Dear Hiroshi,

³   I am happy to hear that you would like to become an architect! Your aunt tells me that you are a good student and a hard worker, so I already know that you'll be able to accomplish whatever you put your mind to.

⁴   You have chosen a difficult but rewarding career. Architecture is unusual because it is a blend of both art and science. You need to be creative to think of new and interesting designs. You also need to be good at math and science so that you can translate your creative ideas into structures that are safe and useful. Even language is important to an architect. You need to be able to express your ideas clearly so that other people can understand them.

⁵   Think about all the different kinds of buildings people need: houses, apartments, schools, office buildings, grocery stores, churches, malls, hotels, factories, gymnasiums, airports, hospitals. Architects figure out the best way to build each building so that it is interesting to look at, safe, and easy to use.

⁶   First, the architect usually creates a proposal that shows the customer his or her idea for the building. If the customer likes it, then the architect keeps working. He or she comes up with a plan that shows all the details of how the building will be constructed. The architect does not actually build the structure. But questions often come up during the construction, so the architect always needs to be available.

⁷   My favorite part of being an architect is seeing the idea that I had in my mind become an actual building. That never stops being exciting for me!

⁸   Please let me know if you have any other questions. You are also welcome to schedule a day to shadow me at work.

Good luck, Hiroshi!

Andrew Daley

1. How do you think Hiroshi was introduced to Mr. Daley?

_____

2. Why does Mr. Daley say that architecture is unusual?

_____

3. What is Mr. Daley's favorite part of being an architect?

_____

4. Name four types of buildings an architect might design.

_____

_____

5. Do you think that Hiroshi and Mr. Daley will ever meet in person? Why or why not?

_____

_____

6. Check the phrase that best describes the author's purpose.

_____ to entertain the reader with a story about how a boy learns what an architect does

_____ to persuade the reader to become an architect

_____ to describe the schooling an architect needs

7. Check the words that describe Mr. Daley.

_____ helpful

_____ kind

_____ unpredictable

_____ intelligent

_____ stingy

8. Why is language important to an architect?

_____

_____

9. How many days did it take Mr. Daley to respond to Hiroshi's e-mail?

_____

On the Mail Trail

What was the Pony Express, and how did it work?

1　Think about the last time you mailed a letter. Maybe you were writing to a grandparent who lives in another state or a friend who moved away. What did you do with your letter? You probably placed it in a mailbox, where a postal carrier picked it up. Eventually, your letter would have traveled by truck or by airplane to its destination.

2　In the 1800s, things were not so simple. The country was expanding westward. After the California Gold Rush, more and more people were moving west. Telegraph lines reached from the East Coast to Missouri, but there was no quick way to get information to California.

3　Then, in 1860, the Pony Express began to transport mail from St. Joseph, Missouri, to Sacramento, California. The Pony Express riders were able to carry mail almost two thousand miles in just 10 days! Then, a boat picked up the mail and carried it to San Francisco.

4　Stations were set up about 25 miles apart between Missouri and California. Each rider would cover about 75 miles a day. The horses could travel about 10 miles per hour, and riders received a fresh horse every 10 or 15 miles. When they changed horses, they would quickly transfer their saddlebags, called *mochilas*, to the new horse.

5　The Pony Express riders were usually young men around 20 years old. They had to be thin and small, because that allowed the horses to travel farther and faster. The riders also had to be willing to risk their lives because the route was so dangerous.

6　Although the Pony Express existed for less than two years, it carried some very

important news. When Abraham Lincoln was elected president of the United States in 1860, the Pony Express riders carried the news west to California. They even alerted the people of California when the Civil War began.

7　By October 1861, the Pony Express was no longer needed. The Pacific Telegraph Company completed its line to San Francisco. The Pony Express was not a success as far as its owners were concerned. It actually lost money in the short time it operated. But the Pony Express remains an interesting piece of American history and an exciting story of the American West.

PONY EXPRESS

ST. JOSEPH, MISSOURI to **CALIFORNIA**
in 10 days or less.

ST. JOSEPH

SACRAMENTO

WANTED

YOUNG, SKINNY, WIRY FELLOWS

Must be expert riders, willing to risk death daily. Wages $25 per week.

APPLY, **PONY EXPRESS STABLES**
St. Joseph, MISSOURI

1. What is a mochila?

   _____

2. Why was the Pony Express originally needed?

   _____

3. Name one important message that was carried to California by the Pony Express.

   _____

   _____

4. Why did Pony Express riders have to be small and light?

   _____

   _____

5. About how long was the route between St. Joseph, Missouri, and Sacramento, California?

   _____

6. Check the line beside the word or words that tell what type of selection this is.
   _____ fiction
   _____ historical nonfiction
   _____ fantasy

7. Number the events below in the order in which they happened in the selection.
   _____ The Pony Express was founded.
   _____ The first rider left St. Joseph on horseback.
   _____ The Pacific Telegraph Company completed its line to San Francisco.
   _____ People began moving to the American West.
   _____ Abraham Lincoln was elected president.

8. *The Pacific Telegraph Company completed its line to Sacramento.* This is the cause. What is the effect?

   _____

9. How does the poster on page 140 add to your understanding of the selection?

   _____

   _____

10. In the 1800s, more and more people were moving westward because of the

   _____.

The Trail West

What will Erik and Alexi find out about the trail of the Pony Express?

1   Erik and Alexi sat at a table at the library after school on Thursday afternoon. The previous day, their class had taken a field trip to visit the Pony Express National Museum in St. Joseph, Missouri. Their homework assignment was to choose something about the museum and the Pony Express that interested them. Then, they were supposed to do some research to find out more about the topic they selected. Erik and Alexi were best friends, and they had decided to work on the project together.

2   "It's hard to pick just one part of our trip that was the most interesting," said Erik.

3   "I know," agreed Alexi. "I think I'd like to learn more about the trail and the route the riders took. We know that they started out right here in St. Joseph. I wonder if it is still possible to follow the trail today."

4   Erik and Alexi used the library's computer catalog to find several books about the Pony Express. One of the books included a map of the route. "This is just what we were looking for!" exclaimed Erik.

5   Alexi looked over Erik's shoulder and pointed to a spot on the map. "After the riders left Missouri, it looks like they traveled through a small part of northern Kansas before they continued into Nebraska. Then, they headed into Wyoming."

6   "Wait," said Erik, pointing to the map. "This part of the route crosses a tiny bit of Colorado first."

7   "You're right," said Alexi.

8   "Look how big Wyoming is," commented Erik. "That must have been one of the longest parts of the trip. I remember our tour guide yesterday saying that some of the roughest terrain and harshest weather was in Wyoming."

9   "Next, the trail passed through Utah and Nevada," continued Alexi. "Finally, the

riders made it to Sacramento!"

10   "Look at this, Alexi," said Erik, opening another book. "It says that there is a group of people who belong to the National Pony Express Association. They live in the seven states that the trail passed through."

11   "Some of them probably live right here in St. Joseph," commented Alexi.

12   "They actually reenact the ride every June," Erik continued. "They dress in authentic clothes, and they try to keep the same schedule that the riders did. One difference, though, is that they use their own horses."

13   "Does each rider travel as far as the original riders of the Pony Express did?" asked Alexi.

14   "No," said Erik. "They only ride about five miles. When they reach the next person, they transfer the mochila. About six hundred people participate!"

15   "The next reenactment is only a month away," said Alexi excitedly. "We'll have to see if our parents will take us there to cheer the riders on."

1. Where did Erik and Alexi's class go on their field trip?

_____

_____

2. Which state does Erik say has rough terrain?

_____

3. How often do the members of the National Pony Express Association do a reenactment?

_____

_____

4. What is one difference between the reenactors and the original Pony Express riders?

_____

_____

5. Check the line beside the word or words that tell what type of selection this is.

_____ biography

_____ fiction

_____ historical nonfiction

Read the phrases below. Write **E** next to the phrase if it describes Erik. Write **A** if it describes Alexi. Write **B** if it describes both Erik and Alexi.

6. _____ says that the trip through Wyoming must have been difficult

7. _____ lives in St. Joseph, Missouri

8. _____ visited the Pony Express Museum the day before

9. _____ wants to cheer on the reenactors as they ride through St. Joseph

10. Which word best describes the boys?

_____ disinterested   _____ curious   _____ worried

11. What does Alexi decide he'd like to learn more about?

_____

12. The trail passes through _____ states.

_____ 3   _____ 5   _____ 7

The Riders of the Pony Express

What was it like to ride the Pony Express?

1   Who were the riders of the Pony Express? They were young men who were adventurous and courageous. They were willing to risk their lives to be a part of the bold new plan to carry mail on horseback from Missouri to California. The trail could be unpredictable. Riders never knew what kinds of problems they might encounter. In the winter, they faced blizzards and blinding snow. Heavy rains could cause some roads to become impassable. There was also the threat of conflict with bandits and Native Americans.

2   There were about 80 Pony Express riders at any one time. They were paid about one hundred dollars a month for their work, which was a large sum, especially for riders who were so young. The youngest rider was said to be only 11 years old, and the oldest was in his 40s. Because the riders had to be lightweight, most of them were very young.

3   Johnny Fry is usually recognized as being the first westbound Pony Express rider. Fry was only 20 years old when he signed up to ride. He weighed less than 120 pounds and was an experienced rider. Fry rode the 80 miles from St. Joseph, Missouri, to Seneca, Kansas. He was able to cover about 12 miles an hour and made it to Seneca without any problems. When the Civil War began, Fry enlisted and fought on the side of the Union. He died in combat in Kansas in 1863. Johnny Fry, pioneer of the Pony Express, was only 23 years old.

4   Buffalo Bill Cody is probably the most well-known rider of the Pony Express. Cody was only 15 years old when he began riding for the Pony Express. Although he was young, he quickly proved himself to be fearless. He was given one of the most dangerous sections of the route through the state of Wyoming.

5   By some accounts, Cody was the rider who completed the longest nonstop ride. The story has it that Cody reached the station where he was supposed to be relieved by another rider. He found that the other rider had been killed, so Cody continued on the route. He rode a total of 322 miles in a little more than 20 hours.

6   Other accounts say that "Pony" Bob Haslam held the record for the longest continuous ride at 370 miles. However, there were few records kept of such information. Much of it was passed along by word-of-mouth, so it is not always easy for historians to know which pieces of information are facts and which have been exaggerated.

7   The one thing that we know for sure is that the young riders of the Pony Express will always be remembered for their unique role in American history.

1. Who was Johnny Fry?

   _____

   _____

2. What sorts of difficulties did riders face on the trail?

   _____

   _____

   _____

3. About how much were the Pony Express riders paid?

   _____

4. Who did Johnny Fry fight for during the Civil War?

   _____

5. Why aren't historians sure who made the longest ride on the Pony Express?

   _____

   _____

Write **T** before the sentences that are true. Write **F** before the sentences that are false.

6. _____ Buffalo Bill Cody started riding for the Pony Express when he was 11 years old.

7. _____ Johnny Fry rode from St. Joseph, Missouri, to Seneca, Kansas.

8. _____ There was the frequent threat of bad weather on the route.

9. _____ Johnny Fry was killed during the Civil War.

10. _____ Most of the Pony Express riders weighed more than 150 pounds.

11. Name three characteristics that were often found in Pony Express riders.

   _____   _____   _____

12. In paragraph 6, it says that information about Pony Express riders was often passed along by "word-of-mouth." Explain what this means.

   _____

   _____

Lone Star Camels

Have you ever heard of the U.S. Camel Corps? Keep reading to learn more about it!

1   When you think of camels, where do you imagine they live? You probably picture them in the deserts of the Middle East, in countries like Egypt or Saudi Arabia. But those are not the only places camels have ever lived. In the second half of the 1800s, a group of camels lived in Texas!

2   How did camels end up so far from their homeland in the Middle East? In 1852, Jefferson Davis, U.S. Secretary of War, recommended that the army try using camels for carrying military provisions in the American Southwest. In 1855, Congress approved the use of $30,000 dollars for the first and only U.S. Camel Corps.

3   Later that year, several U.S. military personnel set sail for North Africa. They had a hard time finding available camels there, so they tried again in Malta, Greece, and Turkey. Finally, after learning much about camels, they landed in Egypt. When their ship sailed for home, it had a number of new passengers, 33 camels and 5 people to care for the animals and show American soldiers how to work with them.

4   The camels were taken to Camp Verde, near San Antonio, Texas. A year later, 41 more camels arrived. Although there were now more than 70 camels in the United States, they were not used often until the Camel Corps was assigned to explore some unfamiliar territory between El Paso and the Colorado River.

5   The camels proved themselves on this trip. They were tougher than the horses and the mules. When the expedition became lost, the soldiers' camels led the people to water. The soldiers were overjoyed. The camels, however, could have continued on for several more days without any water.

6   Even though the camels had proved that they were useful to the military, there were still several problems. Some soldiers did not like the camels at all. They thought the animals were bad tempered. When the camels were irritated or annoyed by something, they reacted by kicking or spitting. They also had a very strong odor that the soldiers did not like. The odor caused other animals that were not used to being around camels to become skittish and upset.

7   Another problem was that the Camel Corps still was not used very often. It was seen as an unnecessary expense for the military. When the Civil War began, the camels were mostly forgotten. Some were sold to places like zoos or circuses. Others were eventually released into the desert.

8   By the mid-1860s, the U.S. Camel Corps no longer existed. Even so, camels still roamed through areas of Nevada, Idaho, Texas, California, and Arizona. The last confirmed sightings were during the early 1900s. Some people claim that camels still live in remote areas of the Southwest desert today, but no one has been able to prove it.

1. What kinds of problems was the U.S. military having with the camels?

   _____

2. Do you think there are any camels still living in the U.S. deserts today? Explain your answer.

   _____

   _____

3. Check the line beside the word or words that tell what type of selection this is.
   _____ fairy tale
   _____ nonfiction
   _____ biography

4. How did the camels help the people when the expedition became lost?

   _____

5. Why did some soldiers dislike the camels?

   _____

6. Number the events below in the order in which they happened in the selection.

   _____ The U.S. Camel Corps no longer existed.

   _____ Jefferson Davis recommended that the army try using camels for transporting things in the desert.

   _____ The last confirmed camel sighting happened in the American desert.

   _____ Members of the U.S. military went to North Africa to look for camels to purchase.

   _____ Another 41 camels arrived in the United States.

Write the words from the article that have the meanings below.

7. stored food and supplies

   _____
   Par. 2

8. extremely happy

   _____
   Par. 5

9. nervous; easily frightened

   _____
   Par. 6

10. faraway; hard to reach

    _____
    Par. 8

One Hump or Two?

Read the following selection to learn more interesting facts about camels.

1   The camel is one of the strangest and oldest creatures living today. Scientists believe that millions of years ago, ancestors of camels lived in North America. There was a bridge of land over the Bering Strait that led to Asia. One group of animals migrated to Asia. These animals developed into the camels of today. Another group migrated to South America. This group developed into the llama, an animal in the same family as the camel.

2   There are two types of camels, the *dromedary* and *Bactrian*. The dromedary has one hump and is found mostly in Arabian countries. The Bactrian camel has two humps and is found in Asian countries. All dromedary camels today are domesticated. Bactrian camels can still be found in the wild in areas of Mongolia and China. The Bactrian camel is shorter and heavier than the dromedary. Also, the pads on its feet are thicker so that it can walk in colder, rockier places than the dromedary.

3   The camel has many interesting characteristics. For example, unlike most animals, it lifts both feet on one side at the same time when it runs. This causes it to rock from side to side when it runs. Another unusual characteristic is the camel's ability to eat almost anything if it becomes hungry enough. It might even eat its own leather harness, part of a tent, or a straw basket if it cannot find the grass it prefers.

4   Camels are the best pack animals in the world. They can carry loads as heavy as 600 pounds 25 miles a day. They can also go without water for as long as two weeks in the winter.

5   You might think that a camel stores extra food and water in its hump or humps. This is what human beings thought for many years, but it is not true. A camel's hump is made of fat and muscle. If a camel has to go without food for several days, it can use the fat in its hump for energy. The camel conserves water in its tissues and cells. Its body does not use the water to cool off the way the human body does. That is why a camel's body temperature can vary, or change, by as much as 11 degrees.

Write **F** before the sentences that are facts. Write **O** before the sentences that are opinions.

1. _____ There are two types of camels.

2. _____ Camels can go without water for long periods of time.

3. _____ Camels are more interesting than horses or mules.

4. _____ A camel's body temperature can vary by 11 degrees.

5. _____ Camels are very strange-looking animals.

6. How did camels travel from North America to Asia millions of years ago?

_____

_____

7. Name one way the dromedary and the Bactrian camel are alike.

_____

_____

8. Name one way the dromedary and the Bactrian camel are different.

_____

_____

9. What is a camel's hump made of?

_____

_____

10. Why does a camel rock from side to side when it runs?

_____

_____

11. What South American animal is the camel related to?

_____

12. Check the words that best describe camels.

_____ hardy _____ stubborn _____ friendly _____ good-natured _____ unusual

13. What is strange about the camel's eating habits?

_____

Survivors in the Desert

How do plants and animals survive in the desert?

1   "I'd like you to think of one thing you could not live without," Mr. Patel told his class. The class was quiet for a moment, and then students began raising their hands. Mr. Patel wrote their answers on the board as the students spoke: *CD players, chocolate ice cream, my bike, computers, pizza, music, my skateboard, movies, weekends, the beach, soccer.*

2   "These are all good answers," said Mr. Patel, turning around to face the class. "Unfortunately, none of them are correct. You all answered my question differently, but the answer I was looking for applies to all of you. Does anybody have any ideas?"

3   Dajuan raised his hand. "Is it water?" he asked.

4   "Excellent!" said Mr. Patel. "Who can tell me why we could not live without water?"

5   "Well," said Gabrielle, "every living creature needs water to survive. I think that more than half of the human body is made of water."

6   "You are right," nodded Mr. Patel. "We are starting our unit about the desert today, and water is scarce in the desert. Plants and animals that live there have had to adapt to those conditions."

7   "Plants have adapted to life in the desert in three different ways," said Mr. Patel. "Some of them have changed their structures. The cactus is one example of this type of plant. It stores water so that it can go for long periods of time without rain. The stem is thick and has a waxy skin, which holds the moisture inside the plant instead of letting it evaporate. The cactus also has spines that give it some shade from the hot desert sun."

8   "Another type of desert plant has adapted by growing very long roots," Mr. Patel continued. This allows it to reach water that is far below the surface of the desert. The third major type of desert plant is dormant during the dryer seasons. This is a sort of sleeping time for plants when they do not continue to grow. It is similar to the way some animals hibernate in the winter. When there is rain and the desert is not so hot, this type of plant comes to life."

9   "What about animals that live in the desert?" asked Carson. "They don't have stems that conserve water or long roots like plants do."

10   "That's true," said Mr. Patel. "But they have found other ways to adapt. Some desert animals are nocturnal. This means that they are only active at night when the desert becomes cooler. During the day, they burrow underground or sleep in caves that are protected from the sun. Some desert animals get moisture from plants. Animals that eat other animals, like vultures, get enough liquid from their food.

11   "After lunch, we'll talk more about life in the desert. You might want to have a big glass of cold water with your lunch. We have a long, dry afternoon ahead of us!" laughed Mr. Patel.

1. What is one way the cactus has adapted to life in the desert?

_____

2. How are a dormant plant and a hibernating animal similar?

_____

_____

3. What do nocturnal desert animals do during the day?

_____

_____

4. How do the long roots of some desert plants help them survive?

_____

5. About how much of the human body is made of water?

_____

_____

6. On the line below, write the words that are dialogue in paragraph 3.

_____

7. Check the sentence that best states the main idea of the selection.

_____ Some desert animals are nocturnal and avoid the most extreme heat of the day.

_____ Mr. Patel's class learns about how plants and animals survive in the desert.

_____ Water is necessary to all forms of life.

Write the words from the story that have the meanings below.

8. not enough of something that is needed

_____
Par. 6

9. change in order to survive in different conditions

_____
Par. 6

10. not active for a period of time

_____
Par. 8

11. active only at night

_____
Par. 10

Answer Key

Write **T** before the sentences that are true. Write **F** before the sentences that are false.

1. **F** Cameron is visiting his grandpa in Massachusetts.
2. **F** Cameron wakes up before Grandpa does.
3. **T** Grandpa makes blueberry pancakes for breakfast.
4. **T** Cameron and Grandpa plan to go fishing in the afternoon.
5. **F** Cameron and Grandpa have to drive to get to the beach.
6. **F** Grandpa finds the tide pool before Cameron does.
7. Name one thing Cameron wants to do when he goes exploring.

   follow the path to the beach, go to the little island, catch fish

Write the words from the story that have the meanings below.

8. changed someone's mind

   convinced   Par. 4
9. talked about

   discussed   Par. 6
10. very small

    miniature   Par. 10
11. ocean water that moves in and out several times a day

    tide   Par. 12
12. not deep

    shallow   Par. 13
13. This story is told in the (first-person, (third-person)) point of view.
14. Do you think Cameron lives near a beach? Why or why not?

    Possible answer: No, because he said if he had these kinds of

    things at home, he might want to get up early.

3

Circle the word that best completes each sentence and write it on the line.

1. Plants and animals must be ___**strong**___ to survive in a tide pool.

   weak   large   (strong)
2. When water dries up, it **evaporates**.

   (evaporates)   dies   melts
3. Starfish and sea urchins have sticky ___**feet**___.

   backs   eyes   (feet)
4. Which type of tide pool is most difficult for animals to live in?

   high-level
5. What is one way humans use kelp?

   as an ingredient in ice cream
6. Check the reason the author probably wrote this story.

   ___ to entertain the reader

   _✓_ to give some facts about tide pools

   ___ to teach people about ocean tides
7. What is the main idea of paragraph 3?

   The saltiness of high-level pools changes, which makes them hard for animals to live in.
8. A barnacle is a ___**a sea animal with a hard shell**___.
9. Why are mid-level tide pools easier for animals to live in?

   The water is deeper there, so the animals don't dry out easily.
10. Have you ever seen a tide pool? If so, describe it. If not, tell what you would hope to find in it.

    Answers will vary.

5

Write **C** before the groups of words that describe Cameron and **G** before the groups of words that describe Grandpa.

1. **G** said that spring and fall are better times for seeing the northern lights
2. **C** thought the northern lights were a spaceship
3. **G** started a fire in the fire pit on the beach
4. **C** wants to move to Maine
5. **G** said blueberries would turn their fingers blue

Write **T** before the sentences that are true. Write **F** before the sentences that are false.

6. **F** Cameron and Grandpa bought some blueberries at the store.
7. **F** Grandpa picked up Cameron's parents at the airport.
8. **T** Dinner reminds Mom of summers in Maine when she was little.
9. **F** Grandpa has never seen the northern lights before.
10. **T** The northern lights are usually seen only in places with high latitudes.
11. Name one thing Cameron and Grandpa do to prepare for Cameron's parents.

    Possible answer: opened windows, did laundry, picked blueberries

Check the meaning of the underlined word in each sentence.

12. Cameron and Grandpa <u>picked</u> two buckets of blueberries.

    ___ chose

    _✓_ gathered
13. Cameron thought the northern lights <u>looked</u> like a spaceship in the sky.

    _✓_ appeared

    ___ stared
14. You can see the northern lights in parts of the world that are closer to the <u>poles</u>.

    ___ long, thin sticks

    _✓_ the most northern and southern ends of Earth

7

Circle the word that best completes each sentence and write it on the line.

1. Some people made up ___**legends**___ to explain the lights they saw in the sky.

   paintings   (legends)   experiments
2. Solar particles and ___**gases**___ collide in Earth's atmosphere to create the northern lights.

   (gases)   light   ice
3. Scientists do not think the northern lights make any ___**sounds**___.

   explosions   steam   (sounds)
4. In Roman myths, who was Aurora?

   goddess of dawn
5. Toward which two areas of Earth does solar wind move?

   the poles
6. About how far away from Earth is the lowest section of the northern lights?

   40 miles
7. Check the sentence that best states the main idea of the selection.

   ___ The northern lights are amazing the first time you see them.

   _✓_ Collisions of solar particles create lights in the night sky.

   ___ The northern lights are also called *aurora borealis*.
8. Why do you think the northern lights can be frightening?

   Possible answer: If you don't know what they are, they might seem mysterious. You might wonder if they were harmful.
9. Why do the northern lights sometimes interfere with TV or cell phone reception?

   The energy from solar wind can get in the way of sound waves or pictures.

9

Answer Key

---

1. Number the events below from **1** to **5** to show the order in which they happened in the story.

   5 Whenever the chief and his son saw the northern lights, they thought of the children playing ball.

   3 The chief and the old man watched the braves play ball.

   1 The boy's parents were worried about him.

   4 The boy asked the chief if he was angry.

   2 The boy followed the trail of the Milky Way.

2. The boy's parents were worried about him because _____

he did not run and play with the other children in the village.

3. How did the boy and the chief get to the Land of the Northern Lights?

They followed the trail of the Milky Way.

4. What were the belts the braves wore made of?

rainbows

5. What do you think the boy taught the children in the Wabanaki village when he got home?

He taught them to play ball.

6. This story is a legend. What elements make a legend different from a regular story?

Possible answer: A legend is not something that actually happened. It may explain something in nature.

7. What natural event does this legend explain?

the northern lights

8. What does the word *brave* mean in paragraph 8? Use the context of the story to help you answer.

a young Native American boy

11

A **fact** is something that can be proven to be true. An **opinion** is what a person believes. It may or may not be true. Write **F** before the sentences that are facts. Write **O** before the sentences that are opinions.

1. **F** Madison's friends are named Drew and Kiona.
2. **O** Thunderstorms are exciting.
3. **F** Madison put some popcorn in a bowl.
4. **F** Drew doesn't know how they will play Mancala without a board.
5. **O** Drew and Kiona will win the game.
6. **O** Mancala All-Stars is a great name for the winning team.
7. Check the sentence that best states the main idea of the story.

      Madison gets bored when it rains.

   ✓ On a rainy afternoon, Malaika teaches some friends how to play an African game.

      Malaika tells her friends about her life in Africa.

8. Where did Drew learn how to play Mancala?

at camp

9. What does the team name the *5Ms* stand for?

Madison and Malaika the Marvelous Mancala Masters

10. What materials will the girls need to play Mancala?

an egg carton, dried beans, markers

11. A **cause** makes something happen. An **effect** is what happens as a result. Write one cause and one effect from the story. **Possible answers:**

Cause: **Rain dotted Malaika's glasses.**

Effect: **She wiped her glasses on her shirt.**

12. Describe a game you like to play on rainy afternoons.

Answers will vary.

13

Circle the word that best completes each sentence and write it on the line.

1. The Chinese tangram is **harder** than it seems.
  easier   older   **(harder)**

2. In the past, the takraw ball was usually made of ___ **rattan** .
  plastic   rubber   **(rattan)**

3. You cannot use your ___ **hands** ___ to hit the ball in takraw.
  feet   shoulders   **(hands)**

4. Check the sentence that best states the main idea of the story.

      Takraw is a popular game in Thailand.

      The Chinese tangram puzzle is not as easy as it may seem.

   ✓ It can be fun and interesting to play games from all around the world.

5. How many shapes is the paper divided into in a tangram?

7

6. What rule of the game makes takraw difficult to play?

You can't use your arms or hands.

Write **J** before the words that describe the United States' version of the game of jacks. Write **T** before the words that describe the Chinese tangram.

7. **J** played with metal pieces

8. **T** possible to make more than 1,500 images

9. **T** begins with a square divided into seven shapes

10. **J** exists in many variations

11. What is the main idea of paragraph 3?

The Chinese tangram is plaed with seven shapes that you use to make different pictures.

12. What is one thing that all the games mentioned in the story have in common?

Possible answer: They are all simple games that can be played with few materials.

15

Write **T** before the sentences that are true. Write **F** before the sentences that are false.

1. **F** Madison wakes up Malaika because she is hungry.

2. **T** Madison's favorite pajamas are pink.

3. **T** Malaika has not made pancakes before.

4. **F** Mom helps everyone make pancakes and eggs for breakfast.

5. Do you think Madison will ask Dad and Malaika to help her the next time she wants to plan a surprise? Why or why not?

Answers will vary.

6. Madison and her dad don't like cracking eggs because _____
they get the shells in the batter

Circle the word that best completes each sentence and write it on the line.

7. Madison's idea for making a surprise breakfast was a ___ **success** .
  mistake   **(success)**   failure

8. Dad thinks that he, Madison, and Malaika work well as a ___ **team** .
  (team)   business   surprise

9. Paragraph 6 contains a simile, a comparison that uses *like* or *as*. Write the simile on the line, and then tell what two things are being compared.

Her fuzzy white slippers peeked out below her pajama pants like two small rabbits; slippers and rabbits

10. What is Malaika's advice for cracking an egg?

Give the egg one good crack.

11. Which adjective best describes Malaika?

      irritable   **✓** helpful   nervous

12. Have you ever surprised someone with a meal you made? If so, tell about it. If not, tell what you would make.

Answers will vary.

17

Answer Key

---

1. Check the reason the author probably wrote this story.
   _____ to show you how to become a chef
   _✓_ to tell about how to make different types of pancakes
   _____ to explain some important rules to remember when you are cooking

2. Number the sentences below to show the order in which you should do each step when you make banana akara.
   _2_ Mash the bananas with a fork.
   _5_ Flip the fritter when the edges turn brown.
   _4_ Coat the skillet with cooking spray.
   _1_ Peel the bananas.
   _3_ Add the nutmeg to the syrup.

3. What will happen if you stir the pancake batter for too long?
   The pancakes will be tough instead of fluffy.

4. Explain how pancakes and banana akara are similar and different.
   Possible answer: They both contain flour and sugar and are fried in a pan.

5. The three tips at the beginning of the selection are all related to
   _✓_ safety. _____ choosing ingredients. _____ cooking for a crowd.

6. Why do you think the bananas in the banana akara recipe need to be very ripe?
   Possible answer: so they are easy to mash

7. What is your favorite special breakfast? List as many ingredients in it as you can.
   Answers will vary.

19

---

1. Number the events below in the order in which they happened in the story.
   _5_ Mrs. Ramirez asked Estéban if he would be interested in fostering a puppy.
   _4_ Estéban said that he missed Sadie.
   _1_ Mrs. Ramirez looked for her keys in her purse.
   _3_ Estéban saw a man with a seeing-eye dog at the mall.
   _2_ Estéban and Mrs. Ramirez went to the mall.

2. Estéban and his mother went to the mall because **he needs new shoes**.

3. Who is Sadie?
   the mutt the Ramirez family adopted when Estéban was a baby

4. Why would the Ramirez family only have a foster puppy for about a year?
   After a year, they would give the dog back to the agency so it could become a seeing-eye dog.

5. A **summary** is a short sentence that tells the most important facts about a topic. Check the sentence below that is the best summary for paragraph 5.
   _____ The chocolate Labrador wore a red harness.
   _✓_ On their way out of the store, Estéban and his mom passed a man walking a dog with a harness.
   _____ Estéban found the shoes he wanted.

Write the words from the story that have the meanings below
6. in a state of great confusion
   chaotic
7. something that fits around an animal's upper body   *Par. 2*
   harness
8. alert; giving a lot of attention to   *Par. 5*
   attentive
9. abruptly; all at once   *Par. 7*
   suddenly   *Par. 10*

21

---

1. Puppies may feel lonely at first because
   most of them have never been away from the other pups in the litter.
2. Why does a foster family need to expose a puppy to lots of different things?
   so it doesn't grow up to be a dog who gets frightened or startled easily
3. Why does Estéban feel worried about giving up a puppy after a year?
   He thinks the puppy will feel like part of the family.
4. Do you think Mr. Crockett will foster more seeing-eye puppies in the future? Why or why not?
   Answers will vary.
5. Check the words that describe Estéban.
   _✓_ responsible
   _✓_ kind
   _____ competitive
   _____ funny
   _✓_ thoughtful
6. Write **F** before sentences that are facts. Write **O** before sentences that are opinions.
   _F_ About half the people at the meeting are thinking about fostering a puppy.
   _O_ Fostering puppies is an enjoyable way to spend time.
   _O_ Estéban and his parents will be a good foster family.
   _F_ The girl sitting across from Estéban has curly hair.
7. What is the setting for this story?
   a classroom at the Seeing-Eye Dog Center
8. What does Mr. Crockett say is helpful when saying good-bye to a foster dog?
   remembering what a gift a seeing-eye dog is
9. Would you be interested in fostering a guide dog? Why or why not?
   Answers will vary.

23

---

1. Check the sentence that best states the main idea of the story.
   _____ Monkeys are fun to have as pets.
   _✓_ Monkeys can be trained to help people with disabilities.
   _____ Monkeys can be mischievous.
2. Name two reasons why monkeys are good at helping humans.
   they are friendly, intelligent, good with their hands
3. Where is Helping Hands located?
   Cambridge, Massachusetts
4. Where do capuchin monkeys live in the wild?
   Central South America

Write **T** before the sentences that are true. Write **F** before the sentences that are false.
5. _F_ Capuchin monkeys live to be about 20 years old.
6. _T_ Capuchin monkeys can learn to perform many different tasks.
7. _F_ Dr. Willard taught capuchin monkeys to speak.
8. _T_ Most monkey owners form a strong relationship with their companions.
9. Why is it important that monkeys have opposable thumbs?
   They can use their hands a lot like humans do.
10. What kind of relationship do most companion monkeys and their owners have?
   _____ distant _____ troubled _✓_ close
11. What is the author's purpose for writing this selection?
   to tell about monkeys that are trained to help people who cannot use their arms or legs

25

Answer Key

27

1. Does a dog or a monkey have a longer "childhood"?
   a monkey
2. Name two tasks the article says that a monkey can do for a person.
   turn on the lights, pick up something
3. How long do monkeys spend in a foster home before they begin their training?
   4–6 years
4. Why do you think it is more common for people to foster dogs than monkeys?
   Dogs are less work. Dogs do not need to be fostered for as long.
5. Check the phrase that best describes the author's purpose.
   ___ to compare different types of monkeys
   ✓ to share information about how companion monkeys are trained
   ___ to convince the reader to get a monkey as a pet
6. Check the sentence below that is the best summary for paragraph 2.
   ___ Monkeys have a longer life span than dogs.
   ✓ Monkeys need time to grow up before they can be socialized as human helpers.

Write the words from the article that have the meanings below.
7. taught how to behave correctly
   socialized Par. 2
8. given something in return for a service or good behavior
   rewarded Par. 3
9. an order
   command Par. 3
10. to finish
    complete Par. 4

29

Circle the word that best completes each sentence and write it on the line.
1. Eliza finished each ___**task**___ the counselors assigned.
   (task) conversation team
2. Annie talked to Eliza after the first ___**practice**___.
   lesson (practice) evening
3. Dad thinks Eliza is a ___**talented**___ soccer player.
   funny (talented) lazy

Write **B** if the sentence describes something that happens before Eliza goes to camp.
Write **A** if the sentence describes something that happens after Eliza gets to camp.
4. _A_ Madeline and Eliza are happy to see that two girls they know are enrolled.
5. _A_ Eliza tells Annie she was nervous.
6. _B_ Dad and Eliza set the table for dinner.
7. _A_ Annie thanks Eliza for helping her stay focused.
8. _B_ Dad tells Eliza that she'll do fine at camp.
9. Do you think Eliza will want to go to camp again next summer? Why or why not?
   Answers will vary.
10. Why does Eliza tell Annie that she felt nervous?
    She doesn't know many people, and she thinks she isn't very quick on the field.
11. Write about a time you tried something new that made you feel nervous at first.
    Answers will vary.

31

1. Number the events below in the order in which they happened in the selection.
   _4_ Pelé was named Soccer Player of the Century.
   _2_ The first soccer clubs were formed in England.
   _1_ Games similar to soccer were played in China.
   _3_ Pelé joined the New York Cosmos.
2. Check the reason the author probably wrote this story.
   ✓ to tell people about the history and popularity of soccer
   ___ to explain how the game of soccer is played
   ___ to show how soccer got its name
3. Name two European countries where soccer is popular.
   Spain, Italy, Germany
4. What do you need to play a game of soccer?
   a ball and two goals
5. In what country was Pelé born?
   Brazil
6. It took longer for soccer to be accepted in the United States because
   A different kind of football was already being played here and people were not eager to try something new.
7. How long ago were games similar to soccer first played in China?
   2,000 years ago
8. The game that Americans call soccer is referred to as ___**football**___ in many other countries.
9. What is the World Cup?
   a worldwide soccer competition that is held every four years
10. Describe what you like or dislike about the game of soccer.
    Answers will vary.

33

Write **T** before the sentences that are true. Write **F** before the sentences that are false.
1. _F_ Mia Hamm was born in Chapel Hill.
2. _T_ Mia's brother's name was Garrett.
3. _T_ Mia is happy to be a role model for young athletes.
4. _F_ Mia wanted to take ballet lessons when she was younger.
5. _T_ Mia helped her team win a gold medal in the 1996 and 2004 Olympics.
6. Why did Mia start the Mia Hamm Foundation?
   to raise money to fight bone marrow disease and to support sports programs for girls
7. Explain why Mia might enjoy being a role model for girls.
   She likes to help other young athletes achieve their goals; there are fewer female athlete role models for girls
8. Why do you think Mia Hamm has been so successful in her life?
   Answers will vary.
9. Check the sentence that best states the main idea of the selection.
   ___ Mia Hamm liked playing soccer better than taking ballet lessons.
   ✓ Mia Hamm is a talented athlete and a giving person.
   ___ Mia Hamm helped her college team win the national championship four times.

Write the words from the article that have the meanings below.
10. mark of excellence
    honor Par. 3
11. of two or more countries
    international Par. 6
12. to help or to supply
    support Par. 7
13. reach; accomplish
    achieve Par. 7

Answer Key

35

1. What inspired Mitch to start Peace Is The Goal?
   He heard a Haitian visitor speak about the poor children in Haiti.

2. In paragraph 2, it says that Mitch is an avid fan of soccer. What does this mean? What clues in the text did you use?
   eager and enthusiastic; Possible answer: The article says he
   loves to play the game, watch it, and talk about it.

3. Which words best describe Mitch Arnold?
   _____ stingy   _____ shy   ✓ generous
   ✓ athletic   _____ thoughtless   ✓ determined

4. Why does Mitch call soccer "the world's game"?
   because people love to play it all around the world

5. As a young teenager, how did Mitch earn money to support his organization?
   by babysitting and by working as a referee

6. Peace Is The Goal has donated soccer equipment to kids in more than _____ countries.
   _____ 40   _____ 60   ✓ 100

7. Why do you think Mitch named his organization "Peace Is The Goal"?
   Possible answer: His goal is to spread peace and hope
   around the world, but in soccer, you also score goals.

8. Now that Mitch is an adult, he no longer works with Peace Is The Goal. Is this statement true or false?
   false

9. What is the author's purpose in writing this selection?
   to tell about a young man and the organization he started

10. If you could start your own charity, who or what would you want to help? Explain.
    Answers will vary.

37

Circle the word that best completes each sentence, and write it on the line.

1. At the farm, the school bus turned onto the ___gravel___ driveway.
   smooth   concrete   (gravel)

2. Uncle Luis's farm is in Northern ___California___.
   Maine   (California)   Arkansas

3. Tomás is Ms. Hallowell's ___student___.
   teacher   (student)   parent

4. Check the phrase that best describes the author's purpose.
   _____ to convince the reader to buy apples only from California orchards
   _____ to explain how to buy and run your own orchard
   ✓ to tell a story about a class trip to an orchard

5. Name two types of apples Uncle Luis grows at Applecreek Orchards.
   Granny Smith, Braeburn, Pink Lady

6. Do you think Uncle Luis will take a vacation next winter? Why or why not?
   Answers will vary.

7. Which word best describes the students in Ms. Hallowell's class?
   _____ creative   _____ bored   ✓ excited

8. Describe what kind of climate apple trees like.
   rainy springs, warm summers, and cool, crisp nights

9. Why do you think apples might need to be shipped to places like Florida?
   Possible answer: The climate isn't right to grow apples there.

10. Why do the apple trees need to be pruned?
    It helps them stay healthy and grow better in the spring.

39

1. Why is Tomás spending the weekend with his uncle?
   to help him set up the fruit stand

2. Do you think Tomás will help Uncle Luis again? Why or why not?
   Answers will vary.

3. What does Tomás remind his uncle to bring to the farmers' market?
   money to make change and a scale

4. What does Tomás get for breakfast? What does he plan to exchange for his breakfast?
   cinnamon buns, apples

Write **T** before the phrases that describe Tomás and **L** before the phrases that describe Uncle Luis.

5. __L__ forgot to load the scale into the truck
6. __T__ traded apples for cinnamon buns
7. __L__ said that your days often start before dawn when you are a farmer
8. __T__ waved to his mom in the driveway

9. Which category best describes this story?
   _____ science fiction   ✓ realistic fiction   _____ biography

10. Find the simile (a comparison using like or as) in paragraph 8. Write it on the line below.
    The sky was beginning to turn as pink as cotton candy.

11. Why is Uncle Luis surprised when Tomás returns his money?
    He thought he would have to pay for breakfast. He didn't
    know that Tomás would make a trade.

12. What does Uncle Luis mean when he says that your days often start before dawn when you are a farmer?
    As a farmer, there are lots of things that need to be done first
    thing in the morning.

41

Write **T** before the sentences that are true. Write **F** before the sentences that are false.

1. __F__ Most apple tree blossoms are pale yellow.
2. __T__ The sweet smell of the flowers attracts bees.
3. __T__ Bees do not like to be out in bad weather.
4. __F__ A Red Delicious apple seed will always produce a Red Delicious tree.
5. __F__ There are about 3,500 varieties of apples around the world.

6. Why do apple farmers purchase bees?
   to help pollinate their trees

7. How do bees carry pollen from one flower to another?
   on their wings

8. What is the name of the process apple farmers use to produce the type of apple tree they want?
   grafting

9. What is a scion?
   the twig from a parent tree

10. Number the following steps in the order in which they occur.
    __2__ The scent of the flowers attracts bees.
    __4__ The bee carries the pollen to another flower.
    __3__ The bee collects nectar from the flower.
    __1__ The apple tree flowers.

Write the words from the article that have the meanings below.

11. loses brightness or color
    fade   Par. 1

12. to draw to itself; to interest
    attract   Par. 1

13. to let go
    release   Par. 2

14. a sweet liquid found in flowers
    nectar   Par. 3

Answer Key

Answer Key

Left column, page 43

1. Number the directions below from **1** to **5** to show the order in which they are listed in the recipe for baked apples.
   - **5** Cover the dish with foil.
   - **1** Preheat the oven.
   - **4** Top each apple with butter.
   - **2** Peel the apples.
   - **3** Spoon the mixture into the hollow core.

Circle the word that best completes each sentence, and write it on the line.

2. You should **refrigerate** any applesauce you do not eat.
   forget (refrigerate) donate

3. Use a wooden spoon to **stir** in the sugar.
   whip squeeze (stir)

4. Spoon part of the **mixture** into the hollow core.
   (mixture) apple cider

5. Why shouldn't you remove the whole core when you make baked apples?
   Leaving a little of the core will hold the juice in.

6. How many ingredients do you need to make baked apples?
   8

7. How long do you need to bake the apples?
   25–30 minutes

8. You can use a fork or a **potato masher** to mash the apples.

9. How does the recipe suggest you serve the applesauce?
   with graham crackers or a spoonful of whipped cream

10. What is your favorite apple dish? If you've cooked with apples before, tell about your experience.
    Answers will vary.

43

Right column, page 45

1. Check the reason the author probably wrote this story.
   - **✓** to tell a story about a girl and her dad and a hike they went on
   - ___ to persuade the reader to hike the Appalachian Trail
   - ___ to tell the reader facts about the Appalachian Trail

2. Check the sentence below that is the best summary for paragraph 7.
   - **✓** Amira's dad tries to make her feel better about the move to Virginia.
   - ___ Amira's dad walked over to the map of Virginia.

3. Do you think Amira will want to go hiking again? Why or why not?
   Answers will vary.

4. Name three things that can be found in Amira's backpack or her dad's backpack.
   Possible answers: bug spray, a water bottle, two granola bars, two oranges, a cell phone, a tree identification guide, sunscreen, a camera

5. Check the words that you think best describe Amira's dad.
   - **✓** athletic
   - **✓** cheerful
   - ___ angry
   - ___ shy
   - **✓** caring

6. Why did hiking make Amira feel better?
   Possible answer: She is enjoying being outside and spending time with her dad.

7. What time of year is it? How do you know?
   the end of summer; Dad mentions that school starts next week.

8. Choose one piece of dialogue from the story, and write it on the line. Tell what the dialogue tells you about the character or the story.
   Answers will vary.

9. If you were trying to cheer up Amira, what would you do or say?
   Answers will vary.

45

Left column, page 47

1. Where did the first section of the Appalachian Trail open?
   Bear Mountain State Park, New York

2. Why can't people carry all the supplies they need with them on the trail?
   The supplies would be too heavy.

3. About how many people hike the entire trail each year?
   450

Write **T** before the sentences that are true. Write **F** before the sentences that are false.

4. **F** The Appalachian Trail goes from Georgia to Ohio.

5. **T** In the 1920s, Myron Avery mapped almost the whole trail.

6. **T** Part of the original Appalachian Trail had to be moved.

7. Check the sentence that best states the main idea of the selection.
   - ___ It takes about six months to hike the entire Appalachian Trail.
   - **✓** The Appalachian Trail, built as a natural escape from city life, is the longest trail in the country.
   - ___ The Appalachian Trail stretches from Springer Mountain, Georgia, to Mt. Katahdin, Maine.

8. Write **C** next to the sentence below that is the cause. Write **E** next to the sentence that is the effect.
   - **E** Parts of the trail would be made into scenic roads.
   - **C** Many people wanted to drive through the countryside and forests instead of hiking.

9. What is a thru-hike?
   hiking the entire trail

A **time line** shows the order in which things happened. Use the time line below to answer the questions that follow.

```
                          trail went from
                          GA to ME
         first section              hurricane destroyed
         of trail opened            part of trail
                    ATC was    Shaffer did
                    founded    first thru-hike
         +----+----+----+----+----+----+----+
         1920    1930    1940    1950
```

10. What happened in 1925?
    The ATC was founded.

11. When did a hurricane destroy part of the trail?
    1938

12. How many years after the hurricane did Shaffer complete the first thru-hike?
    10 years

47

Right column, page 49

1. Why do you think a hiker might be both excited and apprehensive about seeing a bear?
   It is interesting and unusual to see bears in the wild, but the hiker might be worried about his or her safety.

2. Why is it bad to come between a mother bear and her cubs?
   The mother bear might become aggressive.

3. What are two types of poisonous snakes you might see along the trail?
   copperheads   **rattlesnakes**

4. What does the name *armadillo* mean in Spanish?
   little man in armor

5. Check the sentence below that is the best summary for paragraph 4.
   - ___ The armadillo can swim if it has to.
   - **✓** The armadillo is a strange-looking animal that has many ways to protect itself.

6. Why do hikers have to hang their food high in a tree at night?
   so bears can't get it

7. What are the best ways to protect yourself against snakes?
   Wear boots, learn to identify snakes, and don't put your hands and feet in places you can't see.

8. What does the author say about animals in the conclusion of the article?
   If you are quiet and observant, you may get to see animals that most people don't get to see in the wild.

9. If you hiked the trail, what animal would you most like to see? Why?
   Answers will vary.

49

Answer Key

Page 51

1. Why did Sarah and Edie plan to post journal entries and photos?

   so students would be able to check on their progress

2. Do you think Sarah and Edie would recommend this hike to their friends? Why or why not?

   Answers will vary.

3. Do you think Sarah and Edie will go hiking together again? Why or why not?

   Answers will vary.

4. How long did it take Sarah and Edie to complete their hike?

   four and a half months

Check the word that best completes each sentence.

5. Sarah and Edie thought their trip could be a(n) **educational** experience for students.

   ✓ educational ____ normal ____ boring

6. Sarah and Edie were **grateful** for the help of their families and friends.

   ____ annoyed ____ entertained ✓ grateful

7. Bad weather is one **element** of the trip that hikers have to plan for.

   ____ type ✓ element ____ shelter

8. Write one cause from the story and its effect. **Possible answers:**

   Cause: **Sometimes the weather was very hot.**

   Effect: **Sarah and Edie had to drink a lot of water.**

9. Check the character traits that you think would be important for hikers on the Appalachian Trail.

   ✓ athletic ____ shy ____ weak

   ✓ good-natured ✓ knowledgeable ____ irritable

10. Why did Sarah and Edie originally miss a portion of the trail? Why did they go back and hike it later?

    There was a forest fire, so part of the trail was closed. They didn't want to miss hiking any part of it.

51

Page 53

1. Check the phrase that best describes the author's purpose.

   ____ to explain where to look for bears on the Appalachian Trail

   ✓ to tell a story about the tracks a girl and her dad find while hiking

   ____ to persuade the reader to take photos of animal tracks

2. Who do you think would rather see a bear—Amira or Dad? Why?

   Amira because Dad doesn't want to get close to a bear

3. Name two types of tracks Dad and Amira found.

   Possible answers: chipmunk, raccoon, deer, skunk

4. Why did Dad and Amira bring lunch with them?

   so they could spend the whole day in the woods

5. How did Amira use the identification guide?

   She found pictures that looked like the ones she had taken that afternoon

6. Why does Dad say, "Good eyes!" to Amira?

   Amira saw some tiny tracks that Dad would have missed.

7. What activity has helped change how Amira feels about living in Virginia?

   hiking on the Appalachian Trail with her dad

8. How is a digital camera useful in identifying animal tracks?

   You can bring the pictures home to identify them.

9. If you didn't have a camera, how else could you remember what the tracks look like?

   Possible answer: You could sketch them or write down a description.

10. Name several places where you might be able to look for animal tracks near where you live. What kinds of tracks do you think you might see?

    Answers will vary.

53

Page 55

1. What does the phrase *bon voyage* mean?

   happy, safe travels

2. Why will the DiSalvos be moving to France for a year?

   Mr. DiSalvo will be teaching there.

3. Why do you think Jack feels nervous?

   He will be leaving home and moving to another country where he does not speak the language and he does not know anyone.

4. How will Jack and Hannah send answers to their classmates' questions?

   by e-mail

Write **T** before the sentences that are true. Write **F** before the sentences that are false.

5. **F** Hannah and Jack go to Robert Frost Elementary School.

6. **F** The DiSalvos are moving to France for two years.

7. **T** Jack doesn't know what *bon voyage* means.

8. **F** The students are gathered in the gym.

9. In paragraph 2, Ms. Watkins says that Hannah and Jack will have the opportunity to live in France. What does *opportunity* mean in this sentence?

   the chance

10. What is the setting for this story?

    the school cafeteria

11. Write two questions you would ask Hannah and Jack before their trip.

    Answers will vary.

55

Page 57

1. Number the events below from **1** to **5** to show the order in which they happened.

   4 A mountaineer climbed the side of the tower.

   3 The Eiffel Tower was almost torn down.

   1 Alexandre-Gustave Eiffel's design was chosen.

   5 Two people parachuted from the top deck of the tower.

   2 France celebrated its centennial.

2. Why was the Eiffel Tower built?

   to celebrate the centennial of the French Revolution

3. How long did it take to build the Eiffel Tower?

   two years

4. How far does the tower sway on windy days?

   up to five inches

5. Do you think the French will want to tear down the Eiffel Tower in the future? Why or why not?

   Answers will vary.

6. What saved the Eiffel Tower in 1909?

   the invention of the radio

Write the words from the article that have the meanings below.

7. marking the date of something that happened 100 years ago

   centennial

8. the date every year that marks a special event   Par. 2

   anniversary

9. a statue or building that helps people remember something important   Par. 2

   monument

10. a raised surface, like a stage   Par. 2

    platform

57

Answer Key

59

1. Where are the Impressionist paintings located?

   in the Musée d'Orsay

2. What is the name of one of Mom's favorite artists?

   Claude Monet

3. Why does Dad think the family should have a meeting place?

   in case they get separated

4. Do you think Hannah will want to come back to the Louvre on another day? Why or why not?

   Answers will vary.

Write **H** on the line if the phrase describes Hannah. Write **J** if it describes Jack.

5. **J** recognizes Monet paintings from a calendar at home

6. **H** meets a French student named Adrienne

7. **H** tells Mom and Dad where the Impressionist paintings can be found

8. **J** suggests the café as a meeting place

Underline the word that best completes each sentence, and write it on the line.

9. Hannah and Jack **recognize** many of the Impressionist paintings.

   (recognize)   ignore   dislike

10. For a few minutes, Hannah **joins** a group of French students.

    loses   (joins)   admires

An **idiom** is a group of words that has a special meaning. For example, the idiom *hit the hay* means *to go to bed*. Write the idiom from paragraph 17 on the line next to its meaning.

11. stay in a group; not get separated

    stick together

12. Have you ever visited an art museum? If you have, tell about your visit. If you haven't, tell about what types of art you'd like to see.

    Answers will vary.

61

1. What is the name of the river on which the Louvre is located?

   the Seine

2. Do you think the Louvre will grow even larger in the future? Why or why not?

   Answers will vary.

3. Who owns and operates the Louvre today?

   The French government

4. Name one famous piece of art on display at the Louvre.

   Mona Lisa; Winged Victory; Venus de Milo

5. After what major historical event could the public see the art at the Louvre?

   The French Revolution

Write **B** if the sentence describes something that happened before the Louvre opened to the public. Write **A** if the sentence describes something that happened after the Louvre opened to the public.

6. **A** Mitterrand announced a project to expand the Louvre.

7. **B** The French Revolution began.

8. **B** One part of the Louvre protected Paris from the Vikings.

9. **A** I. M. Pei built a glass pyramid for the entrance.

10. **B** The Louvre was turned into a palace.

11. Look at the words *Seine* and *Louvre* in the first paragraph. Why is each of these words followed by a word in parentheses?

    The word in parentheses is the pronunciation.

12. I.M. Pei built a glass pyramid to serve as an entrance to the Louvre. What problem did this solve?

    The problem was that visitors could not tell what was the entrance.

13. How does the photo on page 60 add to your understanding of the article?

    Answers will vary.

63

1. What was the Academy?

   a French government organization with a strict set of rules about art

2. Why didn't Louis Leroy like the paintings of the Impressionists?

   He thought the paintings looked unfinished.

3. Name two Impressionists other than Claude Monet.

   Possible answers: Pierre-Auguste Renoir; Alfred Sisley; Edgar Degas; Mary Cassatt

4. Which came first—frustrated artists were given their own show by the Academy, or Louis Leroy came up with the name *Impressionists*?

   The frustrated artists were given their own show by the Academy.

Write **F** before the sentences that are facts. Write **O** before the sentences that are opinions.

5. **F** The Impressionists challenged ideas about art.

6. **O** It is not fair that artists couldn't create the art they wanted to create.

7. **F** The Impressionists wanted to show movement and light in their paintings.

8. **O** The paintings of the Impressionists look unfinished.

9. **O** Artists should be allowed to have the freedom they need to be creative.

10. Check the sentence that is the best summary for paragraph 4.

    ____ The Impressionists did not think that paintings that looked like photographs were very interesting.

    ✓ Instead of painting realistically, the Impressionists wanted to explore light and movement.

    ____ According to the Academy, all art should look realistic.

65

1. What French word do Hannah and Jack use in the greeting of their e-mail?

   bonjour

2. What is the Tour de France?

   the most famous bicycle race in the world

3. Do you think Hannah and Jack will try more unfamiliar foods while they are in France? Why or why not?

   Answers will vary.

4. Why didn't Mr. DiSalvo go to the top of the Eiffel Tower with his family?

   He doesn't like heights.

5. Check the phrase that best describes the author's purpose.

   ____ to persuade the reader to try *escargots*

   ✓ to tell a story about a family's experiences in France

   ____ to convince the reader to take a trip to Paris

Circle the word that best completes each sentence, and write it on the line.

6. You can see far into the **distance** from the top of the Eiffel Tower.

   height   miles   (distance)

7. Without the butter, the *escargots* would be mostly **tasteless**.

   (tasteless)   rubbery   cooked

8. The French have made the DiSalvos feel **welcome**.

   ignored   (welcome)   friendly

9. In paragraph 5, what does *au revoir* mean? How do you know?

   good-bye; Possible answer: It's at the end of the letter, and the greeting of the letter starts with "hello" in French.

10. How would you describe Jack and Hannah's experience in France so far?

    ____ lonely   ✓ interesting   ____ dangerous

11. After reading this e-mail, do you think you would want to visit France? Why or why not?

    Answers will vary.

Answer Key

1. Check the phrase that best describes the author's purpose.
   _____ to explain why the Tour de France is the most interesting race in Europe
   __✓__ to share some facts about the Tour de France
   _____ to entertain the reader with funny stories about cyclists
2. Check the sentence that best states the main idea of the selection.
   __✓__ The Tour de France is the most difficult and popular bicycle race in the world.
   _____ The Tour de France includes different stages so the riders do not have to bike all night.
   _____ The racers may get to wear different colored jerseys throughout the race.
3. How many cyclists begin the race?
   150
4. Why is the yellow jersey the most important?
   It identifies the leader.
5. Who was the first American cyclist to win the Tour de France?
   Greg LeMond
6. What are two historical events that have interrupted the Tour de France?
   World War I and World War II
7. In paragraph 4, the author says that sometimes the terrain is flat. What does *terrain* mean?
   the land
8. The winner of each stage gets to wear a special **jersey**.
9. Why do you think that only about half the cyclists who start the race make it to the finish?
   Possible answer: It's a really difficult race, and it takes place over a long period of time.
10. Name three qualities that you think a cyclist would need to complete the Tour de France.
    Answers will vary.

67

---

1. Which of the following foods is likely to be high in carbohydrates?
   __✓__ spaghetti _____ lettuce _____ a steak
2. Read the sentences below. Write **F** next to sentences that are facts and **O** next to sentences that are opinions.
   __F__ Meat, eggs, and beans are high in protein.
   __O__ Eating rice and noodles for breakfast is unpleasant.
   __O__ Energy drinks are more satisfying than water after racing.
3. Why do riders have to be careful about drinking too much liquid during a race?
   It can make them slightly heavier. It can cause them to have to work harder.
4. Which meal of the day is usually highest in calories for racers?
   dinner
5. How does your body lose water when you exercise?
   through sweat
6. Why is it important for riders to eat familiar foods and foods they enjoy?
   If they eat things they aren't used to eating, it could make them feel ill.
7. In paragraph 2, it says that racers need food that gives them immediate energy. What does *immediate* mean?
   right away
8. Describe an activity that you need extra energy to do. Do you eat differently when you do this activity?
   Answers will vary.

69

---

1. On what day is Earth Day celebrated?
   April 22
2. Why do you think it is more dangerous for peregrine falcons to live in cities?
   There are more cars and more places for them to get hurt in cities.
3. What is Ben's perfect idea?
   to have a computer that displays the Web cam image of the falcon nest
4. Why does Akiko say that Earth Day seems far away all of a sudden?
   because she is excited about their idea for a table
5. Check the words that describe Ben.
   _____ lonely _____ boring __✓__ excited
   _____ hilarious __✓__ enthusiastic __✓__ creative
6. On the lines below, write a summary for paragraph 1.

   Ben and Akiko's school was having an Earth Day celebration.

Write the idiom from paragraph 3 on the line next to its meaning.
7. to think about something **sleep on it**
8. In paragraph 10, Akiko says that their idea is so original. What does she mean?
   Possible answer: It is a unique idea. No one else will have thought of it.
9. Explain what the school's Earth Day celebration activities all have in common.
   They all have something to do with taking good care of the Earth.
10. Write **C** next to the sentence below that is the cause. Write **E** next to the sentence that is the effect.
    __E__ Ben looked pleased.
    __C__ Akiko said, "Mr. Rashad will love it."
11. Choose one piece of dialogue from the story, and write it on the line. Tell what the dialogue tells you about the character or the story.
    Answers will vary.

71

Write the words from the article that have the meanings below.
1. having babies; reproducing
   breeding
   Par. 1
2. in danger of becoming extinct
   endangered
   Par. 1
3. not in the wild; under someone's control
   captivity
   Par. 2
4. become used to
   adapted
   Par. 3
5. watch closely
   monitor
   Par. 5
6. What caused the falcons' eggshells to become too thin?
   the use of the pesticide DDT
7. How high in the air do falcons make their nests?
   50 to 200 feet in the air
8. How are the places that peregrine falcons nest in the wild similar to the places they nest in cities?
   They are both in high places.
9. Do you think people will continue to help protect peregrine falcons in the future? Why or why not?
   Answers will vary.

Write **T** before the sentences that are true. Write **F** before the sentences that are false.
10. __F__ Only the mother raises the peregrine falcon babies.
11. __F__ DDT is harmless to peregrine falcons.
12. __T__ Peregrine falcons usually mate for life.
13. __T__ Some peregrine falcons are bred in captivity.
14. __T__ Peregrine falcons can fly almost 200 miles per hour.
15. What is one way that humans can monitor peregrine falcons?
    through the use of video cameras
16. Think about what you know about city wildlife. Name another animal that has adapted to life in the city, and explain how.
    Answers will vary.

73

Answer Key

Circle the word that best completes each sentence, and write it on the line.

1. It is not as **dangerous** to learn to fly in natural areas.
   fun (dangerous) interesting
2. Young falcons in ___**urban**___ areas can run into buildings or get hit by cars.
   (urban) country mountain
3. A ___**fledgling**___ is a bird that is learning how to fly.
   falcon (fledgling) volunteer
4. Name one thing for which Salt Lake City is famous.
   the Great Salt Lake; hosting the Olympics
5. How old are the peregrine falcon babies when they begin learning how to fly?
   five or six weeks old
6. Why do the volunteers wear bright orange vests?
   to protect themselves; so they can be easily seen
7. Why do the volunteers work such long hours to help save the young peregrine falcons?
   They know that the work they are doing makes a difference.
8. Check the phrase that best describes the author's purpose.
   _____ to explain why peregrine falcons don't take good care of their babies
   _____ to entertain the reader with a funny story
   _✓_ to tell about a group of volunteers who saved some young peregrine falcons
9. A group of falcon eggs is called a ___**clutch**___.
10. In paragraph 4, why does the author say that the volunteers are right to be worried?
    Only 11 out of 16 babies survived, and almost half of those were helped by volunteers.
11. How do you think the author of the article feels about peregrine falcons? Explain.
    Possible answer: The author cares about peregrine falcons. He/she comments on the work the volunteers do as being worthwhile.

75

---

1. Number the events below from 1 to 5 to show the order in which they happened.
   _3_ Grandpa tells Henry that the fair was about technology and things that were new.
   _1_ Grandpa is pricing things to sell at a yard sale.
   _2_ Grandpa and Henry unroll the poster.
   _5_ Henry says the fair is not like the ones he has visited.
   _4_ Grandpa remembers seeing a television for the first time.
2. What major event in history did the 1939-40 World's Fair follow?
   the Great Depression
3. Why did Americans want something that could give them hope?
   They had been through some hard times.
4. What were the biggest attractions at the fair?
   the Trylon and the Perisphere
5. Why do you think Grandpa says the fair was "a once-in-a-lifetime kind of experience"?
   Answers will vary.
6. How was the 1939 World's Fair different from the fairs that Henry has been to?
   The fair was mostly about technology and things that were new, like TV. The fairs that Henry has been to have rides, games, and fair food.
7. According to Grandpa, what was life like during the Great Depression?
   Life was hard. There was no money for luxuries. Things needed to be reused.
8. Imagine that you are Grandpa, seeing TV for the first time at the fair. Describe your thoughts.
   Answers will vary.

Circle the word that best completes each sentence, and write it on the line.

9. Grandpa ___**attended**___ the 1939 World's Fair in New York.
   forgot (attended) disliked
10. People wanted to see the ___**latest**___ technology at the fair.
    (latest) oldest strangest

77

---

1. Why were World's Fairs first begun?
   to show all of the latest technology in one place
2. Why was it important for Chicago to host the World's Fair in 1893?
   to show the world that Chicago had recovered from the Great Chicago Fire
3. Name two structures that were built for a World's Fair but still exist today.
   Answers will vary.
4. How many countries were part of the largest fair in Missouri?
   62
5. Why did people need to be cheered up after the Great Depression?
   Life had been hard for people during the Depression.

Write F before the sentences that are facts. Write O before the sentences that are opinions.

6. _F_ The Museum of Science and Industry was built in Chicago.
7. _F_ About 50 million people came to see Expo '67.
8. _O_ The St. Louis World's Fair was the most exciting fair.
9. _F_ The 1939 World's Fair had a time capsule.
10. _O_ It is more fun to ride the Ferris wheel than any other amusement park ride.
11. Check the line beside the word that tells what type of selection this is.
    _____ fiction
    _____ fantasy
    _✓_ nonfiction
12. What new technology did many people see for the first time at the World's Columbian Expo in Chicago?
    electricity
13. What was the author's purpose in writing this selection?
    _____ to encourage people to attend World's Fairs
    _✓_ to tell about World's Fairs through history
    _____ to describe the first amusement parks

79

Write the words from the article that have the meanings below.

1. sudden and exciting
   thrill _Par. 1_
2. people who write or study about history.
   historians _Par. 1_
3. well-liked
   popular _Par. 2_
4. no longer used
   abandoned _Par. 3_
5. success and wealth
   prosperity _Par. 5_
6. Which country had the first thrill ride that looped upside down?
   France
7. How many people rode the Mauch Chunk Railway every year?
   35,000
8. What was the name of the first roller coaster in an amusement park?
   Switchback Railway
9. Why were old roller coasters torn down during World War II?
   so the wood and steel could be reused in new ways to help fight the war.
10. Many amusement parks closed during the Great Depression because
    people did not have enough money to go to them.
11. Number the events below from 1 to 5 to show the order in which they happened.
    _2_ A coal-mining company built a tunnel through a mountain.
    _3_ The Switchback Railway opened at Coney Island.
    _1_ The Russians built wooden slides and covered them with ice.
    _5_ Amusement parks in Ohio and California have the most roller coasters.
    _4_ Many amusement parks closed during the Great Depression.
12. Check the sentence that best states the main idea of the selection.
    _____ Roller coasters are popular again, and you do not have to travel far to find one.
    _✓_ People around the world have loved thrill rides for many years and still do today.
    _____ People wanted to have fun and enjoy themselves during the "Roaring Twenties."

81

Answer Key

83

1. Do you think Tess will ask Nonnie to tell her more stories from the quilt? Why or why not?
   Answers will vary.

2. Which piece of the quilt does Tess like best?
   the red flowered block

3. What does Nonnie mean when she says, "This quilt has seen a lot of things"?
   The quilt has been there for many events in her life.

4. How did Nonnie's mother tear her apron?
   rescuing Nonnie's brother from the creek

5. What problem does Tess have at the beginning of the story?
   She is bored because she has been sick for a week.

6. On the line below, write the words that are dialogue in paragraph 12.
   "What about this one?"

7. Check the phrase that best describes the author's purpose.
   ✓ to entertain the reader with a story about a girl who learns about her grandma's quilt
   ___ to explain how to make a quilt at home
   ___ to tell the reader facts about Nonnie's childhood

   Write the idiom from paragraph 3 on the line next to its meaning.

8. not feeling well **under the weather**

9. *Tess's grandma is coming to stay with her for the day. This is the effect.*
   What is the cause?
   Tess's mom had to go back to work.

10. Tell about something that you or your family owns that has a story behind it.
    Answers will vary.

85

1. How did Turkish soldiers use quilted material?
   They wore it under their armor.

2. What is a patchwork quilt?
   a quilt made of many tiny pieces of fabric sewn together in pretty patterns

3. What is a quilting bee?
   a gathering of people who help each other with their quilts

4. Why were quilts practical?
   They used up scraps of material. They kept people warm.

5. What historical event was Susan B. Anthony a part of?
   women's right to vote

6. How can a quilt tell a story?
   It can have images of a family. It might be made up of pieces of clothing that have stories behind them.

7. Check the sentence that best states the main idea of the selection.
   ___ A quilt is made of two pieces of fabric with a layer of batting sewn in between.
   ___ Quilting bees were a good place for women to socialize while they were still doing useful work.
   ✓ Quilts, which are both beautiful and practical, were a way for women throughout history to reuse scraps of material to make something useful.

8. *All quilts are still made by hand today.* Is this sentence true or false?
   false

9. The author of this selection is ___ the history of quilts   .
   ✓ enthusiastic about   ___ bored by   ___ confused by

10. What favorite scraps of fabric would you want to include in a quilt? Explain what they mean to you.
    Answers will vary.

87

1. Check the sentence below that is the best summary for paragraph 4.
   ✓ Some people think that patterns like the log cabin, the wagon wheel, the bear's paw, and the star were used to tell secret codes.
   ___ The bear's paw told the slaves to walk north over the mountains.

2. What was the Underground Railroad?
   It was the name used for the route that slaves took north.

3. What did a star pattern on a quilt mean?
   It meant the slaves should follow the North Star.

4. Why did the slaves want to travel north?
   They wanted to live in freedom.

5. Why don't historians know for certain whether the quilts were used by slaves to communicate information about escaping?
   None of the quilts have survived long enough to prove the stories. The stories were not written down.

6. Do you think the mystery of the slave quilts will be solved in the future? Why or why not?
   Answers will vary.

7. What is oral tradition?
   passing things down by word-of-mouth

8. Why do you think oral tradition is less reliable than writing things down?
   Possible answer: As people tell each other things, some of the details may get changed or left out.

   Circle the word that best completes each sentence, and write it on the line.

9. Quilts may have been used to pass **information** to other slaves.
   (information)   generations   patterns

10. None of the quilts **survived** long enough for historians to study.
    agreed   (survived)   proved

11. Some historians have **different** ideas about the purpose of the quilts.
    few   studied   (different)

89

Write the words from the article that have the meanings below.

1. to happen in turns; every other one
   alternate
   Step 1

2. full of importance
   meaningful
   Step 2

3. place in a particular order
   arrange
   Step 3

4. figure out; decide
   determine
   Step 5

5. Check the phrase that best describes the author's purpose.
   ___ to persuade the reader that quilts are difficult to make
   ✓ to explain how to make a paper quilt
   ___ to tell about the history of quilts

6. Name two ideas of pictures you could include in your quilt.
   Answers will vary.

7. How big should the squares of paper be?
   4-inch squares

8. What information should people be able to get by looking at your quilt?
   the story your quilt tells about you

9. Number the steps below from 1 to 5 to show the order in which they appear in the selection.
   3 Decorate your squares of paper.
   2 Decide what type of quilt to make.
   5 Attach the rows of squares using tape or glue.
   4 Arrange the squares on a table.
   1 Gather the materials you will need.

10. Check the line beside the word or words that tell what type of nonfiction selection this is.
    ___ biography
    ✓ how-to text
    ___ history

11. What do you need to do before you glue the squares together?
    arrange them in a nice order

12. A quilt (or paper quilt) can tell a story about you. What other kind of craft or artwork can tell a story about the person who made it?
    Answers will vary.

Answer Key

Write **F** before the sentences that are facts. Write **O** before the sentences that are opinions.

1. __O__ Uncle Frank's band was the best jazz band of the century.
2. __F__ Devon is helping Uncle Frank clean the attic.
3. __O__ Devon should learn how to play the trumpet.
4. __F__ Uncle Frank's band played at Missouri jazz clubs.
5. __F__ Aunt Clara was in the same band as Uncle Frank.

Write **D** before the phrases that describe Devon and **F** before the phrases that describe Uncle Frank.

6. __D__ sneezes because of the dust in the attic
7. __D__ has never played the trumpet before
8. __F__ thinks Aunt Clara had a beautiful voice
9. __F__ has not played the trumpet in many years
10. __D__ holds up a stack of records
11. What do you think Uncle Frank means when he says, "Once the jazz bug bites you, there's no going back"?

    Once you like listening to or playing jazz music, you will always like it.
12. What does Devon want to do when he hears the music on the records?

    tap his toes or drum his fingers on the coffee table
13. Do you think Devon will learn to play the trumpet in the future? Why or why not?

    Answers will vary.
14. Find the simile in paragraph 11, and write it on the lines below.

    as smooth as honey
15. Write the idiom from paragraph 14 on the line next to its meaning.

    something extra; a bonus **icing on the cake**

91

Circle the word that best completes each sentence below, and write it on the line.

1. In a horn, the longer the sound has to go, the __lower__ the note will be.
   higher   louder   (lower)
2. __Wider__ bells produce a softer sound.
   (Wider)   Narrower   Older
3. The trumpeter has to __vibrate__ his or her lips in the mouthpiece.
   place   (vibrate)   stop
4. In what way did people in medieval times use the trumpet to communicate?

   Different sections of the army would use the trumpet to tell each other important information.
5. Why do some trumpeters use a mute?

   to make the sound muffled
6. What kind of sound will a trumpet make if the trumpeter does not push down any valves?

   a higher sound
7. What was one reason the trumpet became recognized as an important musical instrument?

   Valves were introduced, and the trumpet could make a greater variety of sounds.
8. On the lines below, write a summary for paragraphs 2 and 3.

   Trumpets have been used to communicate since ancient times.
9. Early horns were made from the __horns__ of __animals__.
10. Write one cause from the article and its effect. **Possible answer:**
    Cause: **Push down the valves of the trumpet.**
    Effect: **The note will be lower.**

93

---

1. How many children were there in Dizzy Gillespie's family?
   9
2. What instrument did Charlie Parker play?
   saxophone
3. Name one thing that was different about bebop.
   Possible answer: It moved more quickly; the notes flowed with an irregular pattern.
4. Why was Dizzy's trumpet bent?
   Someone had once accidentally fallen on it.
5. How do we know that Dizzy cared about social causes?

   He did some work for the United Nations. He was a civil rights activist.

Read the phrases below. Write **D** next to the phrase if it describes Dizzy, write **C** if it describes Charlie, and **B** if it describes them both.

6. __D__ born in South Carolina
7. __C__ played the saxophone
8. __B__ made bebop popular
9. __D__ played a bent trumpet
10. Check the sentence that best states the main idea of the selection.
    __✓__ Dizzy Gillespie was a talented musician and a caring person.
    ____ Dizzy Gillespie was the youngest of nine children.
    ____ Dizzy Gillespie played with saxophonist Charlie Parker.
11. Check the words that describe Dizzy Gillespie.
    __✓__ talented   ____ frustrated   __✓__ caring
    ____ shy   ____ anxious   __✓__ musical
12. Do you think people still listen to Dizzy's music today? Why or why not?

    Answers will vary.

95

---

1. Why is America called a "great melting pot"?

   Different cultures of America's citizens combine to make one diverse culture.
2. What are two adjectives the author uses to describe the blues?
   sad   hopeful
3. What two things helped jazz become known around the country?
   railroads   phonographs
4. What sorts of sounds does a singer who is scatting make?
   nonsense sounds that are like the music an instrument would make
5. How did jazz help end segregation?

   The white bandleader Benny Goodman hired an African American pianist and guitarist.

Write **T** before the sentences that are true. Write **F** before the sentences that are false.

6. __F__ The blues are a type of railroad car.
7. __F__ The 1940s were known as the Jazz Age.
8. __T__ Many African American men worked for the Pullman Company.
9. __F__ At first, jazz was mostly played in Georgia.
10. __T__ Ella Fitzgerald was a famous scat singer.
11. Explain what improvising is.

    Improvising is taking a basic melody and then interpreting it yourself, or making it your own.
12. The author's purpose for writing this article was
    ____ to entertain the reader.
    ____ to persuade the reader to listen to jazz.
    __✓__ to inform the reader about the history of jazz.

97

Answer Key

Page 99

1. Check the phrase that best describes the author's purpose.

   ____ to persuade the reader to learn how to play a musical instrument

   _✓_ to entertain the reader with a story about a boy watching his uncle perform

   ____ to explain how to play the trumpet

2. Name two things that were in the picnic lunch Mom packed.

   Answers will vary.

3. Why does Will think Uncle Frank might be nervous?

   He has not played in public in a long time.

4. Why has Uncle Frank started playing the trumpet again?

   He missed playing music and being surrounded by people who love it.

5. Why do you think Devon grins at his mom and Will at the end of the story?

   He felt happy to see his uncle play the trumpet, and he couldn't wait to learn to play like his uncle.

6. Check the words that you think describe Devon.

   _✓_ curious

   _✓_ excited

   ____ stingy

   _✓_ supportive

   ____ angry

   ____ impatient

7. What do the musicians do when they are warming up?

   Getting ready to begin.

8. Number the following events from 1 to 4 to show the order in which they occurred.

   _2_ Devon and Uncle Frank cleaned out the attic.

   _4_ The bandleader tested the microphone.

   _1_ Mom saw Uncle Frank and Aunt Clara perform.

   _3_ Uncle Frank realized how much he missed playing music.

99

Page 101

1. What happens if a person touches the leaves of the sensitive plant?

   The leaves fold up.

2. What is another name for the sensitive plant?

   mimosa

3. Where does the Venus flytrap grow in the wild?

   in North and South Carolina

4. How does the Venus flytrap know that an insect has landed on it?

   It uses its trigger hairs.

5. Do you think Beatriz and Abby will visit the conservatory again? Why or why not?

   Answers will vary.

6. Check the sentence below that is the best summary for paragraph 11.

   ____ The Venus flytrap lives in the Carolinas.

   _✓_ The Venus flytrap attracts and captures insects and small animals.

   ____ The Venus flytrap has sensitive trigger hairs.

Read the sentences below. Write **A** next to the sentence if it describes Abby. Write **B** if it describes Beatriz.

7. _A_ Her brother had a Venus flytrap.

8. _B_ She didn't know that plants could move.

9. _B_ The Venus flytrap is her favorite.

10. _A_ The sensitive plant is her favorite.

Write the words from the story that have the meanings below.

11. a greenhouse where plants are grown and displayed

   conservatory _Par. 1_

12. rose very high in the air

   towered

13. easily affected by something _Par. 3_

   sensitive

14. from a particular place _Par. 6_

   native

101

Page 103

1. Check the phrase that best describes the author's purpose.

   ____ to show that terrariums are the best type of gardens to have

   ____ to tell the history of terrariums

   _✓_ to explain how to assemble and care for a terrarium

2. What kind of a container can you use to make a terrarium?

   a large glass or plastic jar with a lid; a fish bowl covered with plastic wrap

3. Why don't you have to water the plants in a terrarium very often?

   The lid keeps moisture from escaping. The water gets recycled.

4. Name two types of plants that do well in terrariums.

   Possible answers: small ferns; moss; violets; baby tears; begonias

5. What kind of light will your terrarium need?

   a bit of sunlight, but not direct sun or complete shade

6. What can happen if you put too much water in a terrarium, and you do not take off the lid to let some of the water evaporate?

   The plants can rot.

7. In paragraph 1, the text says, "After you water the plants the first time, the moisture will evaporate and then condense on the sides of the container." What does *evaporate* mean?

   It will become part of the air.

8. What can you do if your plants start getting too large?

   You can trim them or move them to a larger terrarium.

9. Would you like to have a terrarium? Explain why or why not.

   Answers will vary.

103

Page 105

1. Where is the United States Botanic Garden located?

   in Washington, D.C.

2. Name two things plants provide for people.

   possible answers: food; shelter; medicine; fuels

3. Who was Admiral Wilkes?

   He led the expedition to the South Seas.

4. Why do you think that different categories of plants are located in different areas at the U.S. Botanic Garden?

   They need to have different types of environments.

5. How can plants help save people's lives?

   Some plants are used to make life-saving medicines.

6. Do you think the U.S. Botanic Garden will continue to grow and preserve new kinds of plants? Why or why not?

   Answers will vary.

Write the idiom from paragraph 6 on the line next to its meaning.

7. have the solution **hold the key**

Write **F** before the sentences that are facts. Write **O** before the sentences that are opinions.

8. _F_ Plants provide the oxygen we breathe.

9. _O_ The most interesting plants are the ones in the Desert House.

10. _F_ Admiral Wilkes led the expedition to the South Seas.

11. _F_ The *Brighamia insignis* grows in Hawaii.

12. _O_ The orchid is the most beautiful type of plant at the U.S. Botanic Garden.

13. Describe a garden you've visited. It can be a botanical garden or the garden in your grandparents' backyard. What kind of plants did it have?

   Answers will vary.

105

Answer Key

107

1. For what is the titan arum best known?
   for having the smelliest flower

2. Where does the titan arum grow in the wild?
   Sumatra, Indonesia

3. Why do you think people are so eager to see the titan arum?
   It is very rare and unusual.

4. The next time a titan arum blooms in the United States, do you think people will line up to see it? Why or why not?
   Answers will vary.

5. Why does the titan arum smell so awful?
   It has to attract the insects that will pollinate it.

6. Check the sentence that best states the main idea of the selection.
   ____ The bloom of the titan arum lasts only one or two days.
   ____ The titan arum grows in the rain forests of Sumatra, Indonesia.
   ✓ The titan arum is fascinating because it is rare, and it is the largest and smelliest flower in the world.

Write T before the sentences that are true. Write F before the sentences that are false.

7. **F** The titan arum can be found growing in the wild all around the United States.

8. **T** Both male and female flowers exist in the center spike of the titan arum.

9. **T** The titan arum has an awful odor.

10. **F** The bloom of the titan arum can last for two to three weeks.

Write the words from the article that have the meanings below.

11. come in contact with
    encountered _Par. 1_

12. a smell
    odor _Par. 2_

13. a sample that is used for scientific study
    specimen _Par. 3_

109

Circle the word that best completes each sentence below, and write it on the line.

1. Dad **gathers** the family for a meeting.
   (gathers) commands requests

2. Mom **records** everyone's vacation ideas.
   changes (records) ignores

3. Dad thinks that going someplace new would be a(n) **adventure**.
   journey (adventure) mistake

4. Name two things Dad says the family could do in Florida.
   Possible answers: swim in the ocean; eat fresh seafood; collect shells

5. Do you think the Garzas will be happy with their decision to camp at Yellowstone? Why or why not?
   Answers will vary.

6. How can you tell that Dad wants to go to the beach?
   He is wearing a sun visor, sunglasses, flip-flops, and a Hawaiian shirt.

7. What problem are the Garzas trying to solve in the story?
   where they should go on their vacation

Read each phrase below. Write M if it describes Maria. Write J if it describes Juan.

8. **J** has a friend named Sophie who went camping

9. **M** guesses that Dad wants to go to the beach

10. In the last paragraph, what do you think unanimous means? What detail in the story helped you figure it out?
    everyone agrees; Possible answer: Dad, Juan, and Maria all raised their hands.

11. What is the setting for this story?
    the Garzas' dining room

12. If you could choose a family vacation spot, what would you choose? Why?
    Answers will vary.

111

Write B next to the sentence if it happened before the Garzas had chosen their books and met at the table. Write A if it happened afterward.

1. **A** The Garzas left the library.

2. **B** Mom and Juan made a list of call numbers.

3. **B** Dad scanned books about Wyoming and national parks.

4. **B** Mom and Juan spread out books on a table.

5. **A** Maria said that they should bring layers of clothes to wear.

Circle the word that best completes each sentence below, and write it on the line.

6. Sophie's family would **loan** the Garzas a tent.
   (loan) borrow sell

7. The materials were **divided** into categories.
   removed explained (divided)

8. Check the sentence that best states the main idea of the selection.
   ✓ The Garzas go to the library to find out how to prepare for their trip to Yellowstone.
   ____ The Garzas agree to meet by the reference desk.
   ____ Juan finds a helpful book that includes different types of checklists.

9. How does park ranger Camilla Jackson suggest campers dress?
   in layers

10. Do you think the Garzas will be well prepared for their trip? Explain.
    Answers will vary.

11. Have you ever been camping? If so, tell about it. If not, tell why you would or would not like to go.
    Answers will vary.

113

Write F before the sentences that are facts. Write O before the sentences that are opinions.

1. **O** Wolves are beautiful creatures.

2. **F** Yellowstone currently has the major predators it had throughout history.

3. **O** Wolves are an annoyance.

4. **F** Wolves mostly hunt elk and deer.

5. **F** More than 400 wolves live in Yellowstone today.

6. What caused the "see-saw" to become unbalanced at Yellowstone?
   Humans interfered with nature.

7. If another species disappears at Yellowstone in the future, what do you think scientists might do?
   Answers will vary.

8. What is a keystone species?
   a species upon which many other plants and animals depend

9. Did the environment at Yellowstone begin to change right before or right after the wolves were brought back?
   right after

10. What problem did some people have with wolves in Yellowstone?
    They thought the wolves were a dangerous annoyance.

11. Based on this selection, how do you think the author feels about wolves at Yellowstone?
    Possible answer: It sounds like the author is glad that wolves are back in Yellowstone and believes that they should be protected.

12. Write one cause from the selection and its effect.
    Cause: **Cause: Wolves hunt elk and deer.**
    Effect: **Effect: Other animals eat the leftover meat.**

Answer Key

115

1. Why do geysers erupt?

   Heated water is trapped deep underground. Eventually the pressure from the hot water underground becomes stronger than the weight of cold water.

2. About how often does Old Faithful erupt?

   every 30 to 90 minutes

3. Name two places other than Yellowstone where geysers can be found.

   Possible answers: New Zealand; Japan; Iceland

4. How far into the air can Steamboat Geyser shoot water?

   350 feet

5. What happens when the pressure of the hot water underground is greater than the cold water on top?

   The geyser erupts.

6. Check the sentence below that is the best summary for paragraph 4.

   _____ The steam in a geyser has nowhere to go.

   ✓ Boiling water and steam build up below the cold water until the pressure is too great and the geyser erupts.

   _____ When a pot boils on a stove, the steam can evaporate.

   Write **T** before the sentences that are true. Write **F** before the sentences that are false.

7. __T__ There are almost 400 geysers at Yellowstone.

8. __T__ After all the pressure is released, the eruption ends.

9. __F__ All geysers shoot water into the air at the same height.

10. Where does the word *geyser* come from, and what does it mean?

    It comes from an Icelandic word that means to *gush*.

11. How do you think Old Faithful got its name? (Hint: Are its eruptions predictable?)

    Possible answer: It erupts on a predictable schedule.

12. How can you see Old Faithful erupting without visiting Yellowstone?

    You can visit the NPS Web cam online.

117

1. Why were the railroad companies happy about the creation of the national parks?

   They wanted more people to travel greater distances so they could make more money.

2. How tall can redwoods grow to be?

   more than 300 feet tall

3. Name one of the national monuments that was created while Theodore Roosevelt was president.

   Petrified Forest; The Grand Canyon

4. Do you think more national parks will be founded in the future? Why or why not?

   Answers will vary.

5. Number the events below from 1 to 4 to show the order in which they happened.

   __1__ George Catlin was concerned about people moving westward.

   __4__ The National Park Service was given the War Department's monuments.

   __2__ Yellowstone National Park was created.

   __3__ Congress passed the Antiquities Act.

6. Many historic sites and battlefields are the responsibility of the __National Park Service__.

7. What is special about the Assateague Island National Seashore?

   Wild horses run freely there.

8. Do you agree with the author that it's important to preserve natural spaces? Explain.

   Answers will vary.

A **time line** shows the order in which things happened. Use the time line below to answer the questions that follow.

Casa Grande Ruin	Antiquities Act
Yosemite State Park	National Park Service Bureau created
Yellowstone National Park	Cape Hatteras National Seashore

1860 1880 1900 1920 1940

9. What year was the Antiquities Act passed? __1906__

10. Which park was created in 1872? __Yellowstone National Park__

11. Was Yosemite or Yellowstone created first? __Yosemite__

119

1. Check the words that describe Max.

   _____ competitive

   ✓ adventurous

   ✓ curious

   ✓ imaginative

   _____ shy

2. Why was Max glad to have Winnie with him on the spacecraft?

   He would feel lonely without her company.

3. What was Max trying to take a picture of when he woke up?

   a massive crater

4. In his dream, Max thinks he is bobbing up and down in the air as he is trying to snap a photo. What is happening in real life that makes him think this?

   Winnie is prancing around on his waterbed.

5. On the line below, write the words that are dialogue in paragraph 5.

   "Prepare for landing!"

   Write the idiom from paragraph 4 on the line next to its meaning.

6. getting nervous __getting cold feet__

7. How does the picture on page 118 add to your understanding of the story?

   Possible answer: It helps you understand right away that Max is dreaming.

8. Describe the setting in Max's dream.

   Max is on a space ship, and then he lands on Mars.

9. What is the setting for the part of the story that takes place in reality?

   Max's bedroom

   If the event described takes place in reality, write **R** on the line. If it takes place in Max's fantasy, write **F** on the line.

10. __R__ Winnie was trying to let Max know it was time for her breakfast.

11. __F__ Max took a picture from the porthole of the spaceship.

12. __F__ Max unsnapped parts of his spacesuit.

13. __R__ Max got out of bed.

14. __F__ Max told Winnie her picture would be in a history book.

121

1. What did Percival Lowell think Schiaparelli saw on the surface of Mars?

   canals

2. What was the name of the American spacecraft that was sent to Mars in 1965?

   Mariner 4

3. Do you think that scientists will continue to look for life on Mars? Why or why not?

   Answers will vary.

4. In the passage, what problem did Percival Lowell have?

   Lowell began the theory that an advanced civilization on Mars had built canals all over the planet. He was wrong because Schiaparelli said there were channels, not canals, on Mars.

5. Does this selection take place in reality, or is it a fantasy? How can you tell?

   The selection takes place in reality. You can tell because the author writes about things that actually happened in history.

6. Check the phrase that best describes the author's purpose.

   _____ to explain why there is no life on Mars

   ✓ to tell about the search for life on Mars

   _____ to persuade the reader to visit Mars someday

   Read each sentence below. If the event took place before 1965, write **B** on the line. If it took place after 1965, write **A** on the line.

7. __A__ *Spirit, Opportunity,* and *Curiosity* landed on Mars.

8. __B__ Schiaparelli noticed lines that ran across the surface of the planet.

9. __B__ Lowell created the theory about canals and civilization on Mars.

   Write the words from the article that have the meanings below.

10. an expert in the study of the universe

    astronomer   Par. 2

11. watching closely

    observing   Par. 2

12. ahead of its time

    advanced   Par. 3

Answer Key

Left column, page 123:

1. What is the first thing you need to do if you want to become an astronaut?
   get a college education
2. What was the profession of most of the first astronauts?
   pilot
3. Why do you need to be in good shape to be an astronaut?
   Space flight is hard on the human body.
4. Why do you think astronauts need to be good communicators?
   Possible answers: They work in teams. It is important for reasons of safety.
5. What is a simulator?
   a computer game that looks and feels like the inside of the shuttle
6. On the lines below, write a summary for paragraph 4.
   To be an astronaut, you should be educated in the sciences, be in good physical shape, and be a trustworthy person.
7. Write **T** before the sentences that are true. Write **F** before the sentences that are false.
   F New astronauts can fly as soon as they have finished their training.
   T Today, astronauts need to be able to perform many tasks.
   F Alan Shepard was the oldest astronaut to go into space.
   F If you fly 40 miles above Earth, you are officially in space.
   T You need to have good eyesight to be a shuttle pilot.
8. Name characteristics that an astronaut needs to have.
   Possible answer: An astronaut needs to be in good shape, have good eyesight, be a good communicator, be trustworthy, and be reliable.
9. **John Glenn** was the first American to orbit Earth.
10. Do you think you would make a good astronaut? Why or why not?
    Answers will vary.

123

Right column, page 125:

1. Check the words that describe Amelia.
   ____ funny
   ✓ brave
   ✓ determined
   ____ suspicious
   ✓ proud

Circle the word that best completes each sentence, and write it on the line.

2. Mom and Maggie helped Amelia **overcome** her fear of the water.
   ignore (overcome) explain
3. Maggie **enjoys** Amelia's company.
   (enjoys) dislikes forgets
4. Amelia's dad had not **expected** her to learn so much in one afternoon.
   wanted (expected) selected
5. Why does Maggie feel sad at the beginning of the story?
   She doesn't think Amelia will come over to swim, and nothing is as much fun without Amelia.
6. What does Dad mean when he says, "I'm going to have a prune for a daughter all summer"? **He thinks Amelia will be in the water so much that her skin will be wrinkled for much of the summer.**
7. Why does Amelia want to learn how to swim?
   She is tired of being scared of the water, and she doesn't want to miss a whole summer of swimming with Maggie.
8. Why does Amelia say that she wants to come back tomorrow?
   She is excited that she is learning how to swim.

Find the simile in paragraph 4, and write it on the line below.

9. **swims like a dolphin**
10. Why did it make a difference that Amelia was finally ready to learn?
    Possible answer: She was never going to learn until she was ready and decided she wanted to learn.
11. Tell about something that you tried, even though it made you uncomfortable at first.
    Answers will vary.

125

Left column, page 127:

Circle the word that best completes each sentence, and write it on the line.

1. Salt water is **denser** than fresh water.
   (denser) colder deeper
2. Something that is **heavier** than the same volume of water will sink.
   older (heavier) stronger
3. The Dead Sea is **saltier** than the oceans of the world.
   lighter fresher (saltier)
4. Check the phrase that best describes the author's purpose.
   ✓ to explain how to conduct two experiments about floating
   ____ to persuade the reader to become a scientist
   ____ to show why the water in the Dead Sea is so salty
5. Why do you think you need to use salt in the second experiment?
   so the salt will dissolve
6. Why does the apple float while the carrot sinks?
   The cells of the apples are not packed as tightly. Because they have more air, they are lighter and float better.
7. What do you think would happen if you used an egg instead of a grape in the second experiment?
   the egg would sink
8. Where is the Dead Sea located?
   near Israel

Write the words from the article that have the meanings below.

9. packed tightly together; heavy
   dense Par. 2
10. able to float
    buoyant Par. 4
11. melts; turns from a solid into a liquid
    dissolves Par. 5

127

Right column, page 129:

1. Name two rainy day activities Teresa and Manuel did.
   Possible answers: played games, painted, made cookies, watched movies, helped their mom clean out closets
2. Why did the grass squish beneath their feet as they walked across it?
   The ground was full of water.
3. Where did Mrs. Lopez hear the news that Sawmill Creek was flooding?
   on the radio
4. If the story continued, what do you think would happen next?
   Answers will vary.
5. Name one way that Teresa and Manuel are similar.
   Possible answers: They are both bored; they both want to play outside; they both think that sandbagging the house is exciting.

Write **F** before the sentences that are facts. Write **O** before the sentences that are opinions.

6. **F** At the beginning of the story, Teresa and Manuel are bored.
7. **O** Keeping the basement from flooding is exciting.
8. **F** Sawmill Creek is rising quickly.
9. **F** Mom and Dad overlap the sandbags so there are not gaps between them.
10. **O** Rainy days are boring.
11. Why does the family need to sandbag the house?
    to keep the basement from flooding
12. Mom hopes that covering the bags with plastic will make them more
    watertight .

129

Answer Key

Page 131

1. Who owned South Fork Dam at the time of the flood?
   South Fork Fishing and Hunting Club

2. Why does the author say that the fact that Johnstown exists today shows the strength of people in that town?
   They didn't let the flood destroy them or their town. They were able to recover from the tragedy.

3. What problem did the people of Johnstown have in the selection?
   The dam burst and water destroyed much of the town and took many lives.

4. Number the events below from 1 to 5 in the order in which they happened.
   2 Some people were worried that the dam might not hold.
   3 The dam sent 20 million tons of water rushing down the Little Conemaugh River.
   5 The Johnstown Flood National Memorial was founded.
   1 The South Fork Fishing and Hunting Club bought the South Fork Dam.
   4 The people of the town were caught by surprise.

5. Check the sentence that best states the main idea of the selection.
   ____ The water flooded Johnstown at speeds of about 40 miles per hour.
   ____ The city of Johnstown is located in southwestern Pennsylvania.
   ✓ The Johnstown Flood in 1889 was one of the worst disasters in American history.

6. Check the line beside the word or words that tell what type of nonfiction selection this is.
   ____ biography
   ✓ history
   ____ how-to text

7. Does this story take place in reality, or is it a fantasy? How can you tell?
   The selection takes place in reality. You can tell because the author writes about things that actually happened in history.

8. What do you think the purpose of the Johnstown National Memorial is?
   to remember the flood and the people who lost their lives

9. The picture on page 130 looks like a black and white photo from a newspaper. How does the artwork help you understand the story better?
   Answers will vary.

131

Page 133

1. What is Hiroshi's homework assignment?
   to decide what kind of career he wanted and to research it

2. What did Hiroshi like about Fallingwater?
   He felt like the house was part of the forest and the waterfall was part of the house.

3. How does Saki tease her brother at the end of the story?
   She reminds him that he wanted to be a clown when he was little.

4. What made Hiroshi want to be an oceanographer?
   He likes that there are so many things humans don't know about the ocean yet.

5. On the line below, write the words that are dialogue in paragraph 4.
   "What are you doing?"

Read the sentences below. Write **H** next to the sentence if it describes Hiroshi. Write **S** if it describes Saki.

6. **S** eats a green apple
7. **H** wanted to be a firefighter
8. **S** has a good memory
9. **H** likes the mystery of the ocean
10. **H** makes a list of career ideas

Write the idiom from paragraph 2 on the line next to its meaning.

11. something that is not likely **a long shot**

12. Do you think it's wise of Hiroshi to choose a more practical career than being a professional baseball player? Explain.
    Answers will vary.

13. If you had to write about a career and research it, what would you choose? Why?
    Answers will vary.

133

Page 135

1. How were the prairie houses similar to the landscape of the Midwest?
   Both are flat and spread out.

2. How do you think Fallingwater got its name?
   It was built on top of a stream and waterfall.

3. What is the shape of the Guggenheim Museum in New York City?
   a spiral

4. What do you think Wright's feelings about the natural world were?
   He probably had an interest in and respect for the natural world.

5. Check the sentence below that is the best summary for paragraph 4.
   ✓ One of Wright's most popular designs was the prairie house, which imitated the Midwest landscape.
   ____ The Midwest contains many areas of flat farmland.

6. Check the words that describe Wright.
   ✓ imaginative   **✓** unique
   ____ talkative   ____ rude
   ✓ creative

7. Check the line beside the word or words that tell what type of selection this is.
   ✓ biography   ____ myth
   ____ how-to

8. Write the sentence that is a caption on page 134.
   Frank Lloyd Wright found inspiration for his buildings in the natural world.

9. *Wright believed that buildings should basically look like boxes with windows.* Is this true or false?
   false

10. A **forest** was the inspiration for Wright's Johnson Wax Company headquarters.

135

Page 137

Write **F** before the sentences that are facts. Write **O** before the sentences that are opinions.

1. **O** Robert Ballard is the greatest living scientist today.
2. **F** Ballard grew up in San Diego.
3. **O** More money should be spent on space exploration than on ocean exploration.
4. **F** The *Titanic* sank on her maiden voyage in 1912.
5. **F** Ballard discovered tubeworms near the Galápagos Islands.

6. What is one way in which outer space and the oceans are similar?
   There are mysteries about both that humans have not discovered yet.

7. Why was Ballard's discovery of deepwater tubeworms so important?
   It showed that a form of life could survive without the sun. This changed the way scientists thought about the possibility of life on other planets.

8. What did *Argo* send back to the surface from deep underwater?
   photographs

9. Why did Ballard have to wait a year before exploring the *Titanic*?
   He had to wait for good weather conditions.

10. Who is the author of the novel *20,000 Leagues Under the Sea*?
    Jules Verne

Write the words from the article that have the meanings below.

11. very interested in
    fascinated _{Par. 1}
12. making a map of
    mapping _{Par. 3}
13. something expensive and pleasurable that isn't really necessary
    luxury _{Par. 6}
14. a device that uses sound waves to find underwater objects
    sonar _{Par. 7}

137

Answer Key

Page 139

1. How do you think Hiroshi was introduced to Mr. Daley?
His aunt probably introduced him.

2. Why does Mr. Daley say that architecture is unusual?
It is a blend of both art and science.

3. What is Mr. Daley's favorite part of being an architect?
seeing the idea that he had in his mind become an actual building

4. Name four types of buildings an architect might design.
Possible answers: houses; apartments; schools; office buildings; grocery stores; churches; malls; hotels; factories; gymnasiums; airports; hospitals

5. Do you think that Hiroshi and Mr. Daley will ever meet in person? Why or why not?
Answers will vary.

6. Check the phrase that best describes the author's purpose.
✓ to entertain the reader with a story about how a boy learns what an architect does
___ to persuade the reader to become an architect
___ to describe the schooling an architect needs

7. Check the words that describe Mr. Daley.
✓ helpful
✓ kind
___ unpredictable
✓ intelligent
___ stingy

8. Why is language important to an architect?
He or she has to be able to express ideas clearly.

9. How many days did it take Mr. Daley to respond to Hiroshi's e-mail?
two

139

Page 141

1. What is a mochila?
a saddlebag that was used to carry mail

2. Why was the Pony Express originally needed?
to get mail from the Midwest to California

3. Name one important message that was carried to California by the Pony Express.
Possible answers: Abraham Lincoln was elected president; the Civil War began

4. Why did Pony Express riders have to be small and light?
so their horses could go farther and move faster

5. About how long was the route between St. Joseph, Missouri, and Sacramento, California?
about 2,000 miles

6. Check the line beside the word or words that tell what type of selection this is.
___ fiction
✓ historical nonfiction
___ fantasy

7. Number the events below in the order in which they happened in the selection.
2 The Pony Express was founded.
3 The first rider left St. Joseph on horseback.
5 The Pacific Telegraph Company completed its line to San Francisco.
1 People began moving to the American West.
4 Abraham Lincoln was elected president.

8. *The Pacific Telegraph Company completed its line to San Francisco.* This is the cause. What is the effect?
The Pony Express was no longer needed.

9. How does the poster on page 140 add to your understanding of the selection?
Answers will vary.

10. In the 1800s, more and more people were moving westward because of the
California Gold Rush

141

Page 143

1. Where did Erik and Alexi's class go on their field trip?
Pony Express National Museum

2. Which state does Erik say has rough terrain?
Wyoming

3. How often do the members of the National Pony Express Association do a reenactment?
once a year

4. What is one difference between the reenactors and the original Pony Express riders?
Possible answers: They use their own horses; they only ride about five miles.

5. Check the line beside the word or words that tell what type of selection this is.
___ biography
✓ fiction
___ historical nonfiction

Read the phrases below. Write **E** next to the phrase if it describes Erik. Write **A** if it describes Alexi. Write **B** if it describes both Erik and Alexi.

6. E says that the trip through Wyoming must have been difficult

7. B lives in St. Joseph, Missouri

8. B visited the Pony Express Museum the day before

9. A wants to cheer on the reenactors as they ride through St. Joseph

10. Which word best describes the boys?
___ disinterested ✓ curious ___ worried

11. What does Alexi decide he'd like to learn more about?
the trail and the route the riders took

12. The trail passes through ___ states.
___ 3 ___ 5 ✓ 7

143

Page 145

1. Who was Johnny Fry?
He was probably the first westbound Pony Express rider.

2. What sorts of difficulties did riders face on the trail?
Possible answers: bad weather; rough terrain; conflict with bandits or Native Americans

3. About how much were the Pony Express riders paid?
one hundred dollars a month

4. Who did Johnny Fry fight for during the Civil War?
The Union

5. Why aren't historians sure who made the longest ride on the Pony Express?
There were few written records. Information was passed along by word of mouth.

Write **T** before the sentences that are true. Write **F** before the sentences that are false.

6. F Buffalo Bill Cody started riding for the Pony Express when he was 11 years old.

7. T Johnny Fry rode from St. Joseph, Missouri, to Seneca, Kansas.

8. T There was the frequent threat of bad weather on the route.

9. T Johnny Fry was killed during the Civil War.

10. F Most of the Pony Express riders weighed more than 150 pounds.

11. Name three characteristics that were often found in Pony Express riders.
Possible answers: adventurous; courageous, young

12. In paragraph 6, it says that information about Pony Express riders was often passed along by "word-of-mouth." Explain what this means.
People tell each other things, but the information is not written down.

145

Answer Key

1. What kinds of problems was the U.S. military having with the camels?
Some soldiers did not like the camels. Also, the Camel Corps still was not used very often.

2. Do you think there are any camels still living in the U.S. deserts today? Explain your answer.
Answers will vary.

3. Check the line beside the word or words that tell what type of selection this is.
_____ fairy tale
✓ nonfiction
_____ biography

4. How did the camels help the people when the expedition became lost?
They led the people to water.

5. Why did some soldiers dislike the camels?
They thought the animals were bad tempered and had a strong odor.

6. Number the events below in the order in which they happened in the selection.
4 The U.S. Camel Corps no longer existed.
1 Jefferson Davis recommended that the army try using camels for transporting things in the desert.
5 The last confirmed camel sighting happened in the American desert.
2 Members of the U.S. military went to North Africa to look for camels to purchase.
3 Another 41 camels arrived in the United States.

Write the words from the article that have the meanings below.

7. stored food and supplies
provisions   Par. 2

8. extremely happy
overjoyed   Par. 5

9. nervous; easily frightened
skittish   Par. 6

10. faraway; hard to reach
remote   Par. 8

147

Write **F** before the sentences that are facts. Write **O** before the sentences that are opinions.

1. **F** There are two types of camels.
2. **F** Camels can go without water for long periods of time.
3. **O** Camels are more interesting than horses or mules.
4. **F** A camel's body temperature can vary by 11 degrees.
5. **O** Camels are very strange-looking animals.

6. How did camels travel from North America to Asia millions of years ago?
on a bridge of land over the Bering Strait

7. Name one way the dromedary and the Bactrian camel are alike.
Possible answers: They run the same way; they both will eat almost anything; both can carry large loads and go for long periods without water.

8. Name one way the dromedary and the Bactrian camel are different.
Possible answers: number of humps; where they are found; body shape and weight; pads on the feet

9. What is a camel's hump made of?
fat and muscle

10. Why does a camel rock from side to side when it runs?
It lifts both feet on one side at the same time.

11. What South American animal is the camel related to?
the llama

12. Check the words that best describe camels.
✓ hardy   ✓ stubborn   _____ friendly   _____ good-natured   ✓ unusual

13. What is strange about the camel's eating habits?
Camels will eat almost anything if they have to.

149

---

1. What is one way the cactus has adapted to life in the desert?
It stores water; the stem is thick and waxy; the spines give a shade.

2. How are a dormant plant and a hibernating animal similar?
They both go through a period where they are in a type of deep sleep.

3. What do nocturnal desert animals do during the day?
sleep

4. How do the long roots of some desert plants help them survive?
They can reach water that is far below the surface of the desert.

5. About how much of the human body is made of water?
more than half

6. On the line below, write the words that are dialogue in paragraph 3.
"Is it water?"

7. Check the sentence that best states the main idea of the selection.
_____ Some desert animals are nocturnal and avoid the most extreme heat of the day.
✓ Mr. Patel's class learns about how plants and animals survive in the desert.
_____ Water is necessary to all forms of life.

Write the words from the story that have the meanings below.

8. not enough of something that is needed
scarce   Par. 6

9. change in order to survive in different conditions
adapt   Par. 6

10. not active for a period of time
dormant   Par. 8

11. active only at night
nocturnal   Par. 10

151

Notes

Notes